Adult Coloring Book
Flowers, Volume 1
A Stress-Relieving Coloring Book

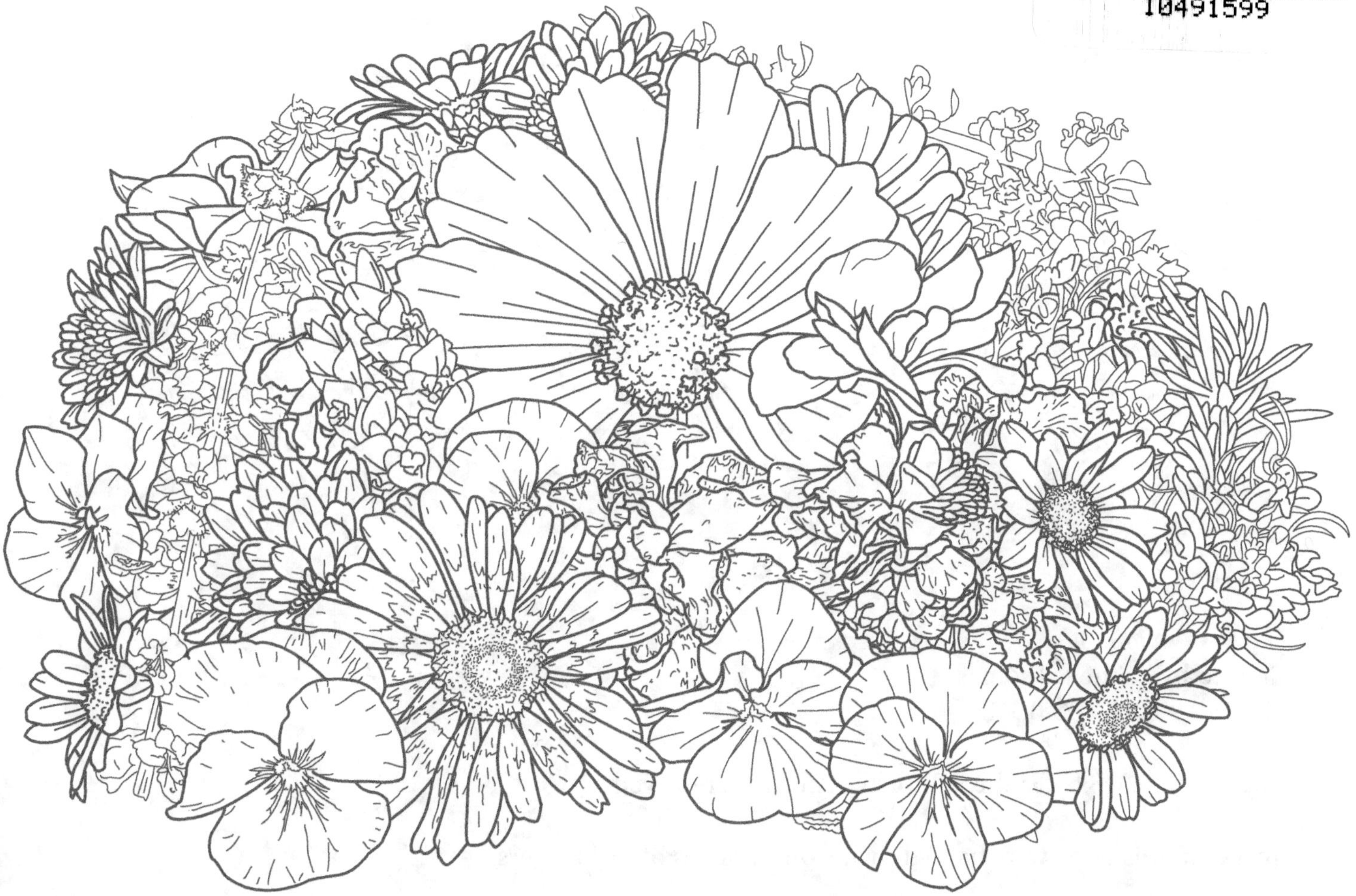

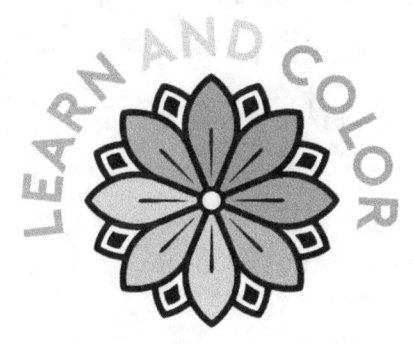

LEARN AND COLOR

Dear Reader,

Thank you for buying *Flowers, Volume 1*. I hope you have fun coloring these flowers.

I enjoy receiving comments and suggestions from readers. Your ideas are always very helpful. I also love to hear how you are using our books.

So, let me know – the good and the bad – and I will try to make these books even better!

Thank you and keep coloring!

Faithe
faithe@learnandcolor.com

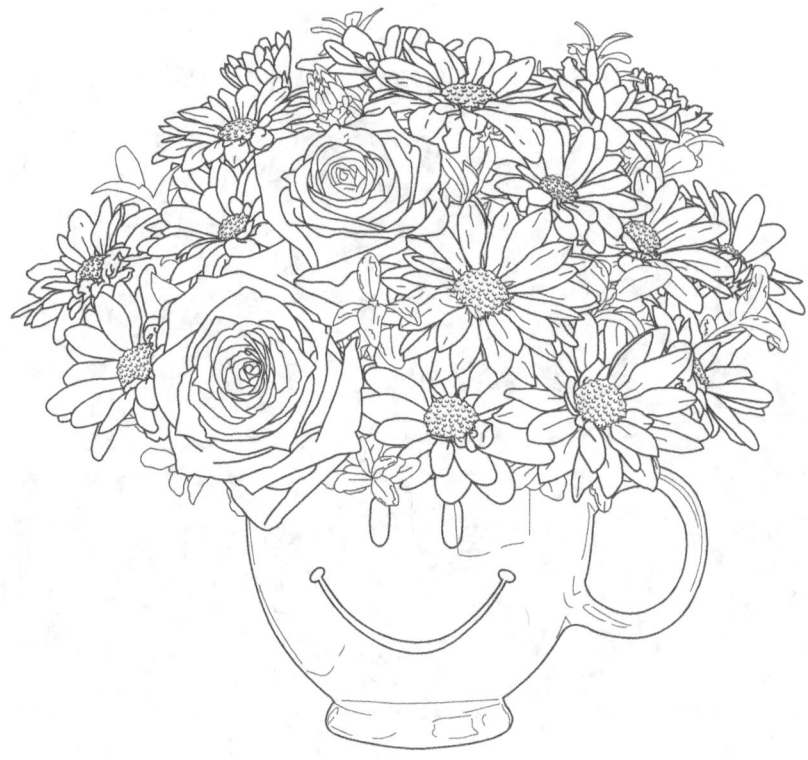

Flowers, Volume 1
Created by Faithe F Thomas
ISBN 978-1-947482-06-7

Images in this book were hand drawn from samples of real flowers.

Published by Learn and Color
   an imprint of Master Design Marketing, LLC
   789 State Route 94 E
   Fulton, KY 42041

Check out all our coloring books at LearnAndColor.com

Sample Pages from Flowers, Volume 1

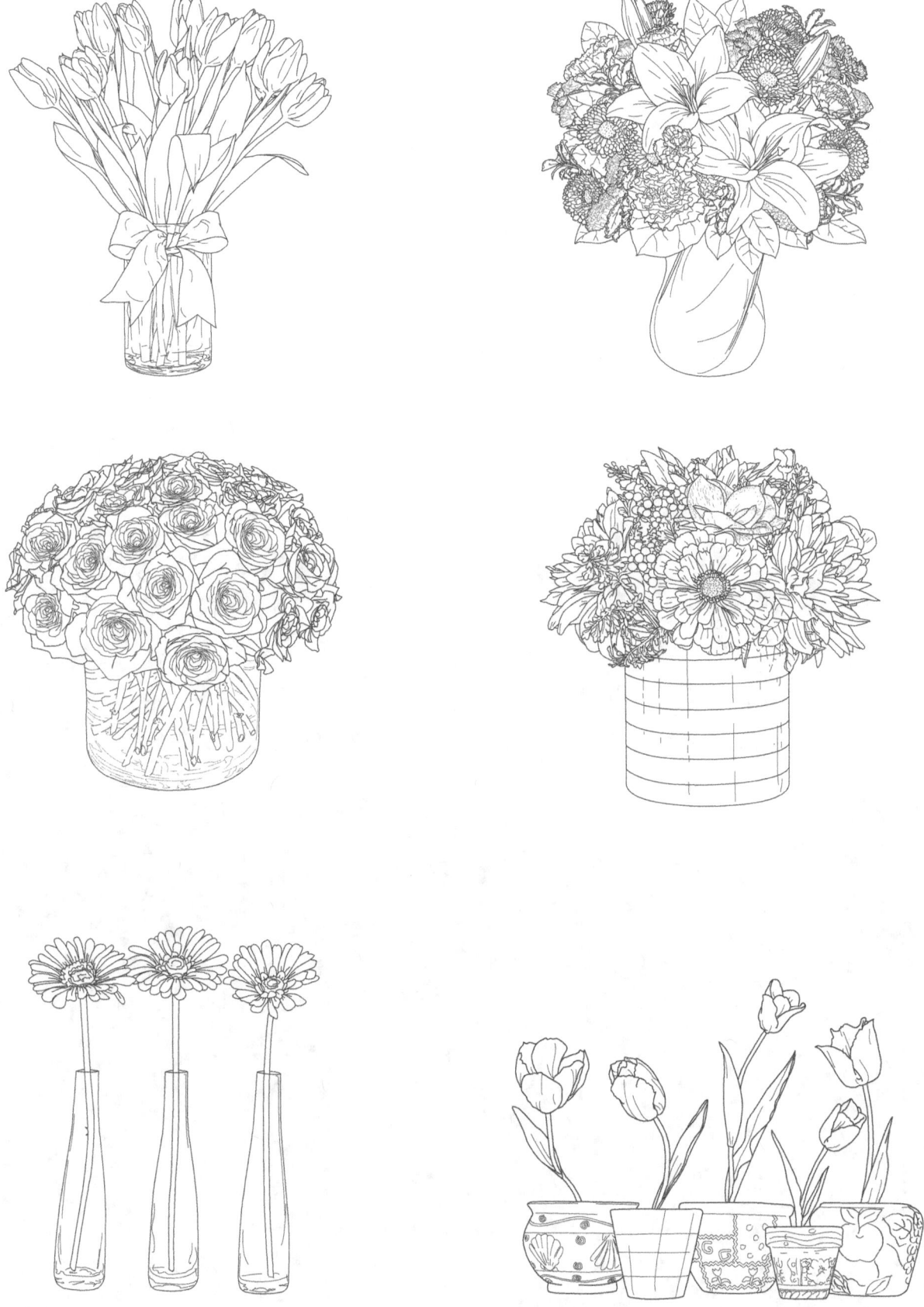

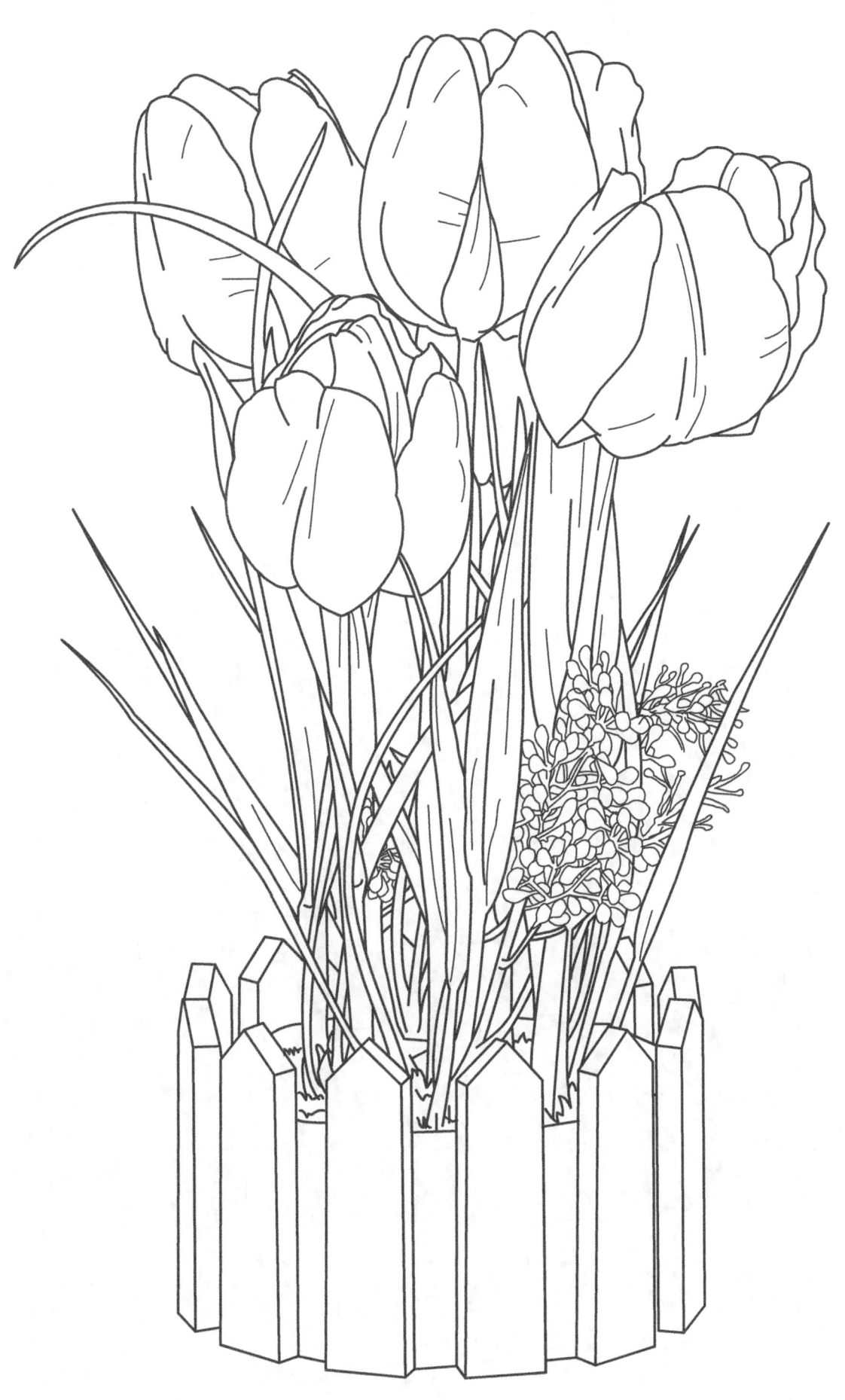

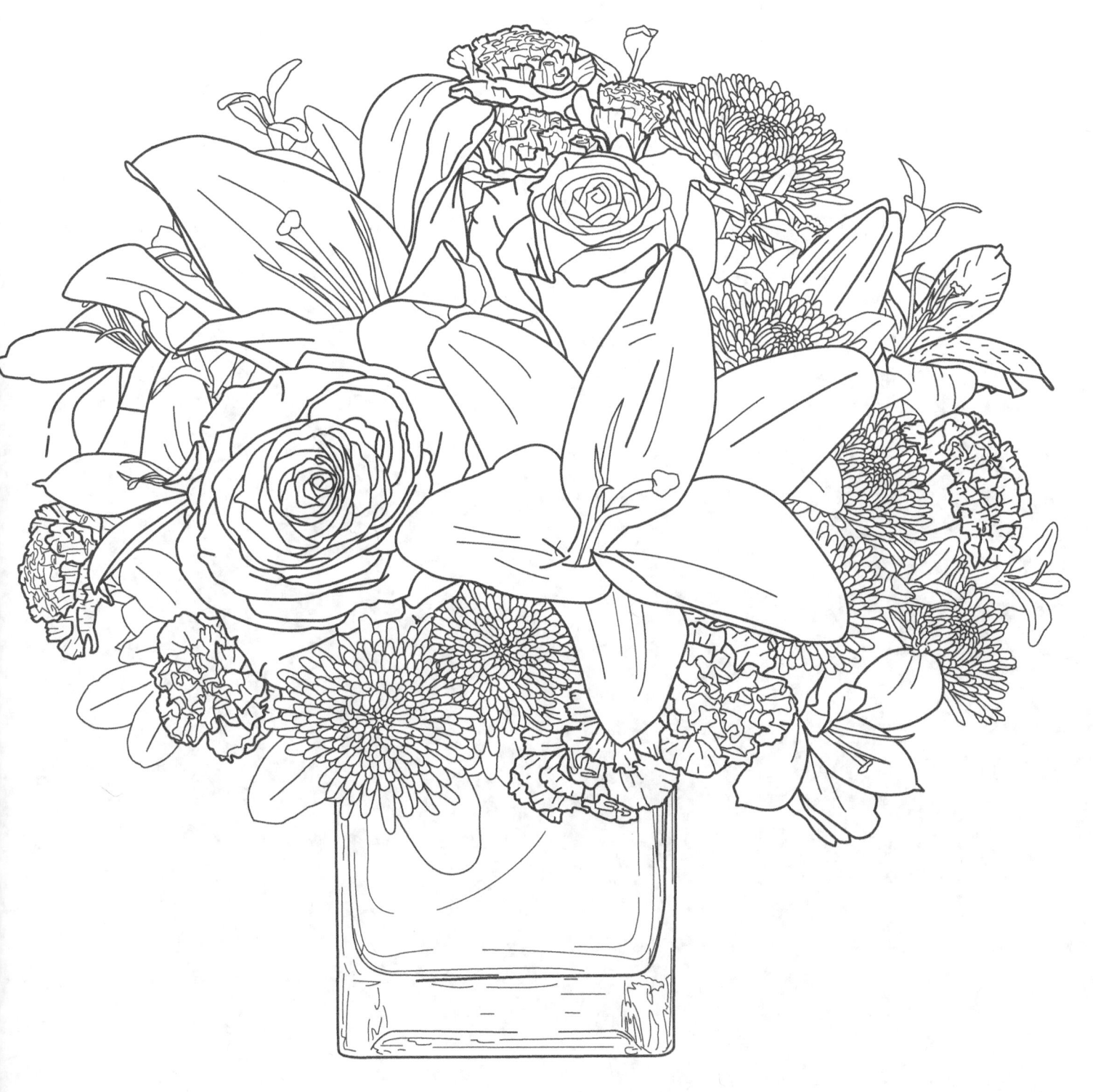

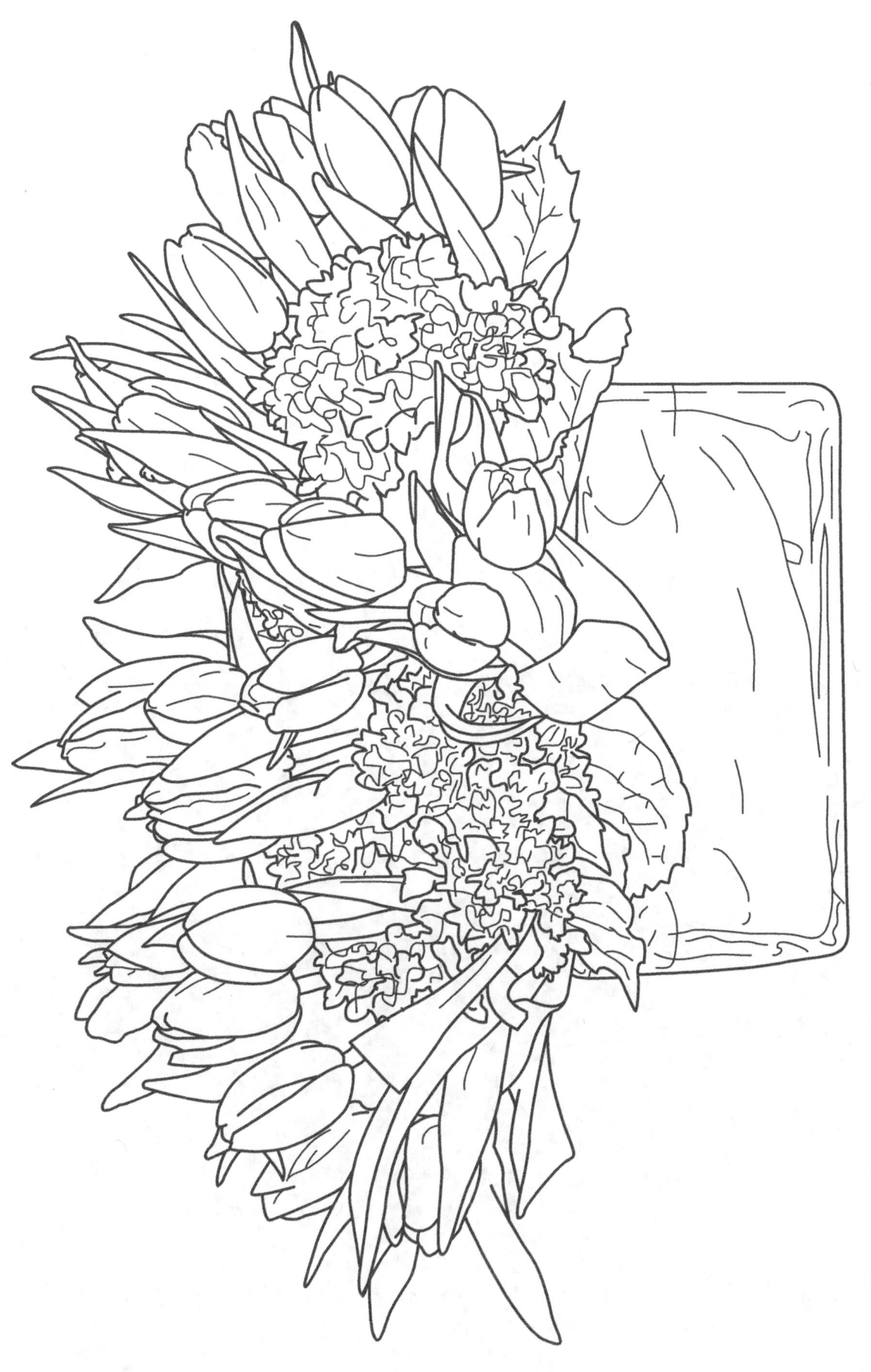

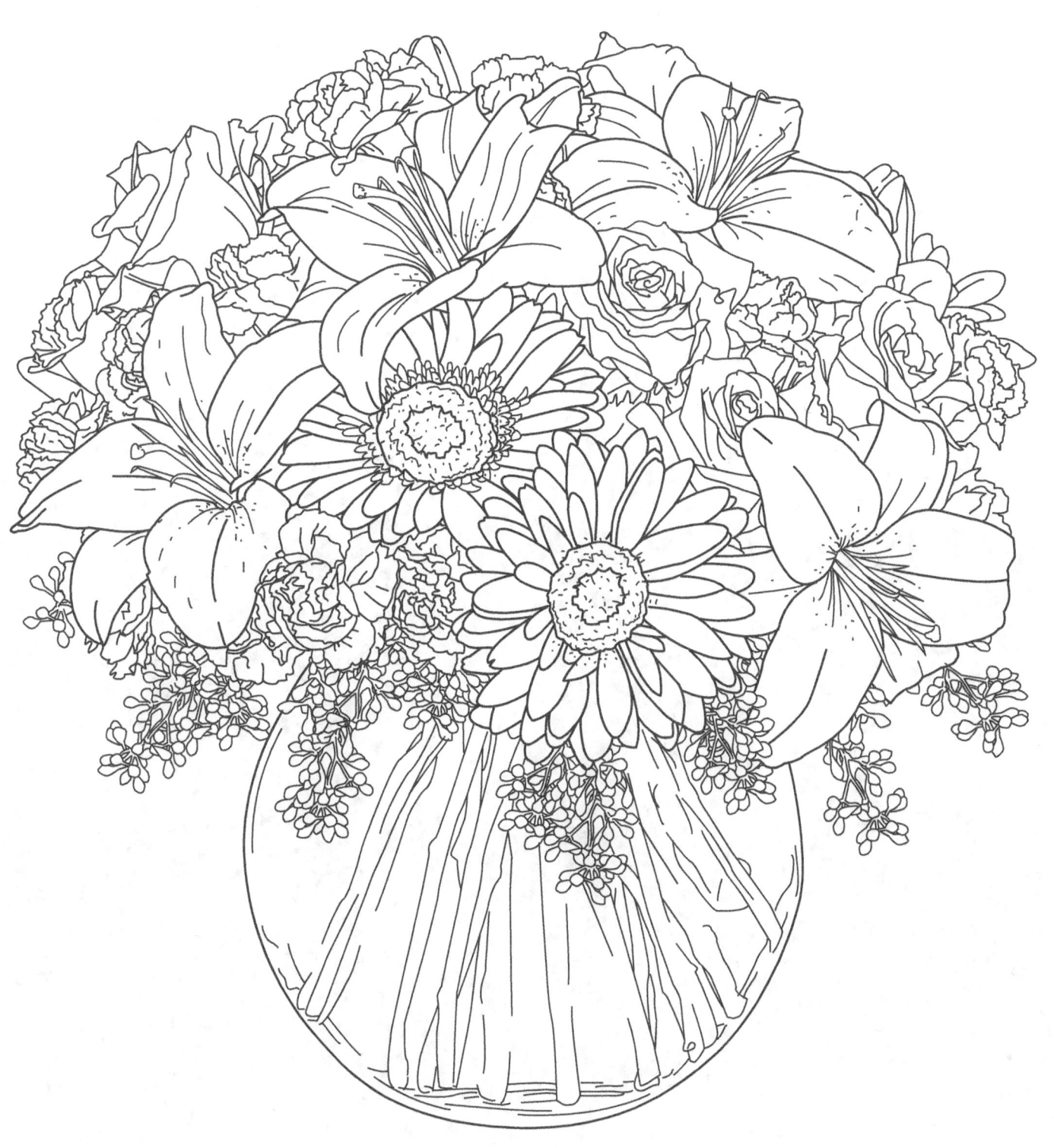

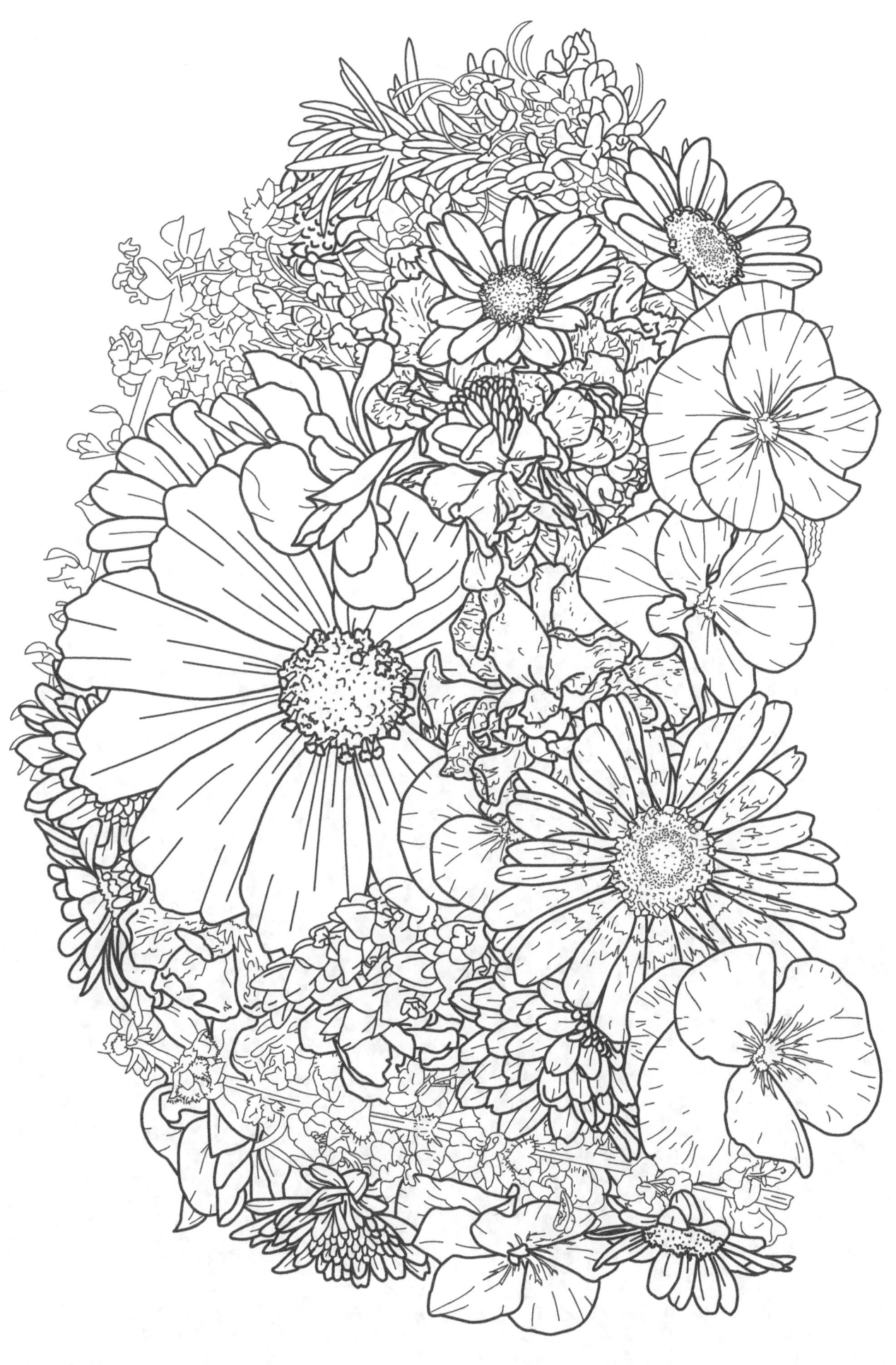

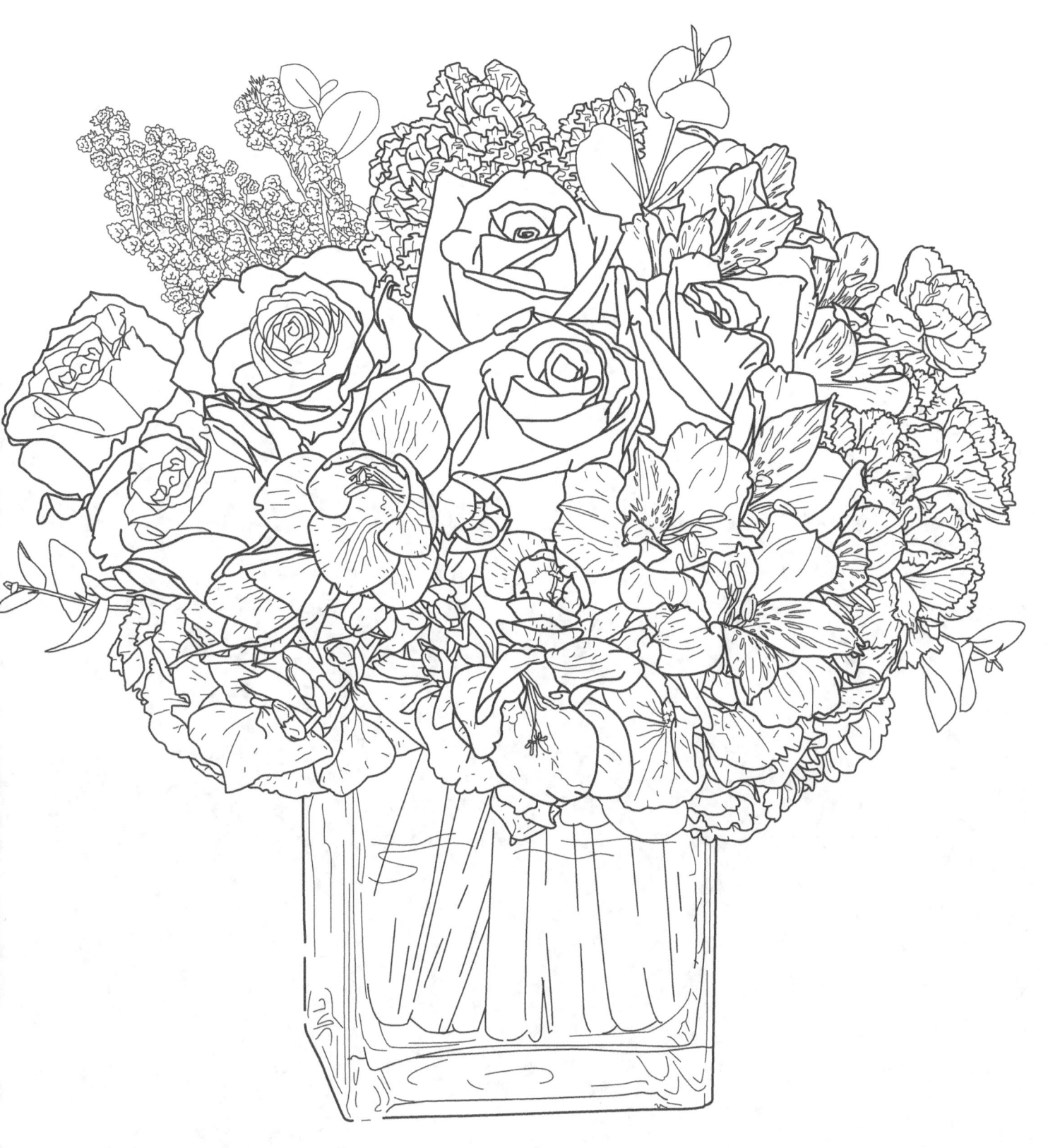

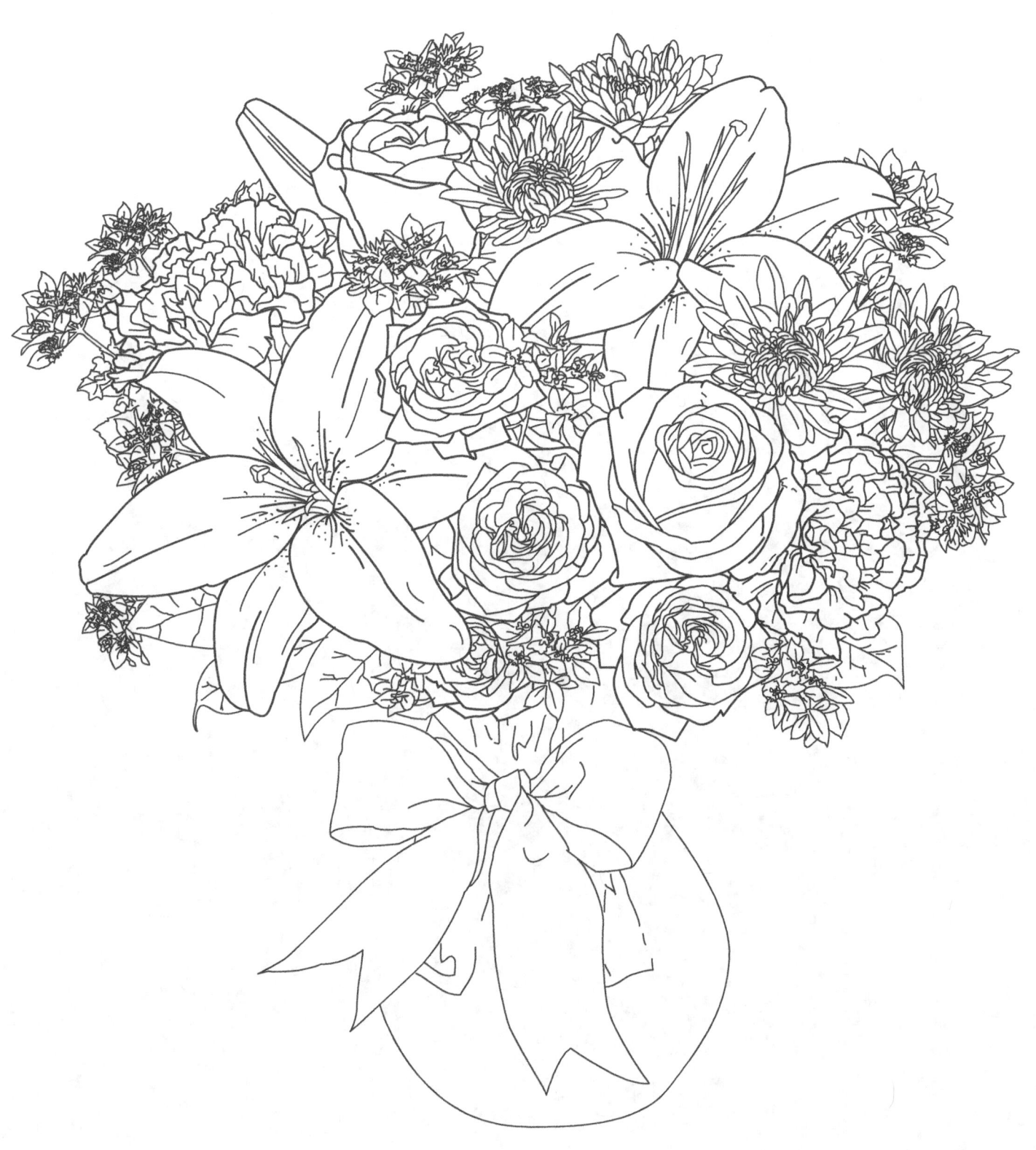

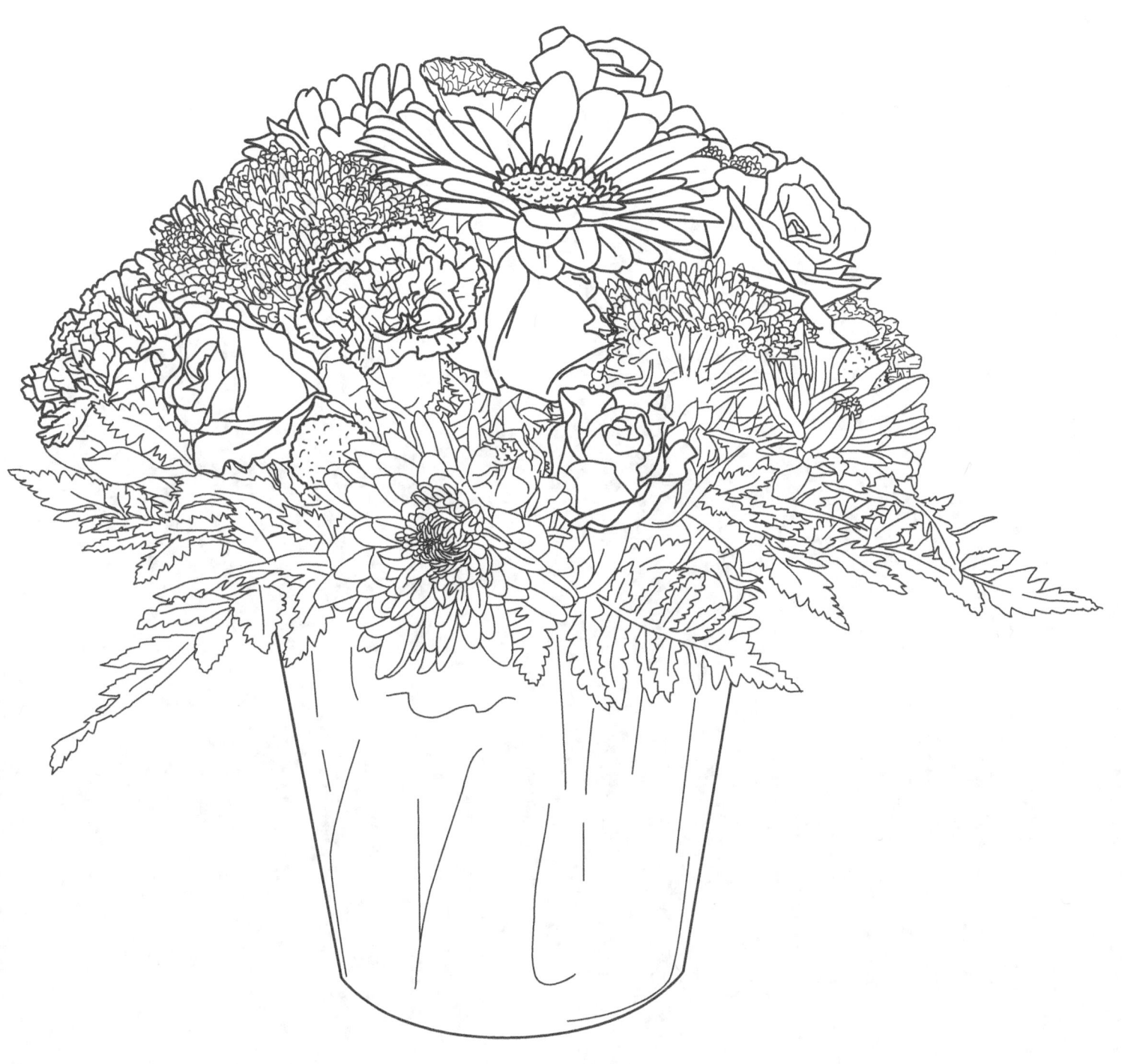

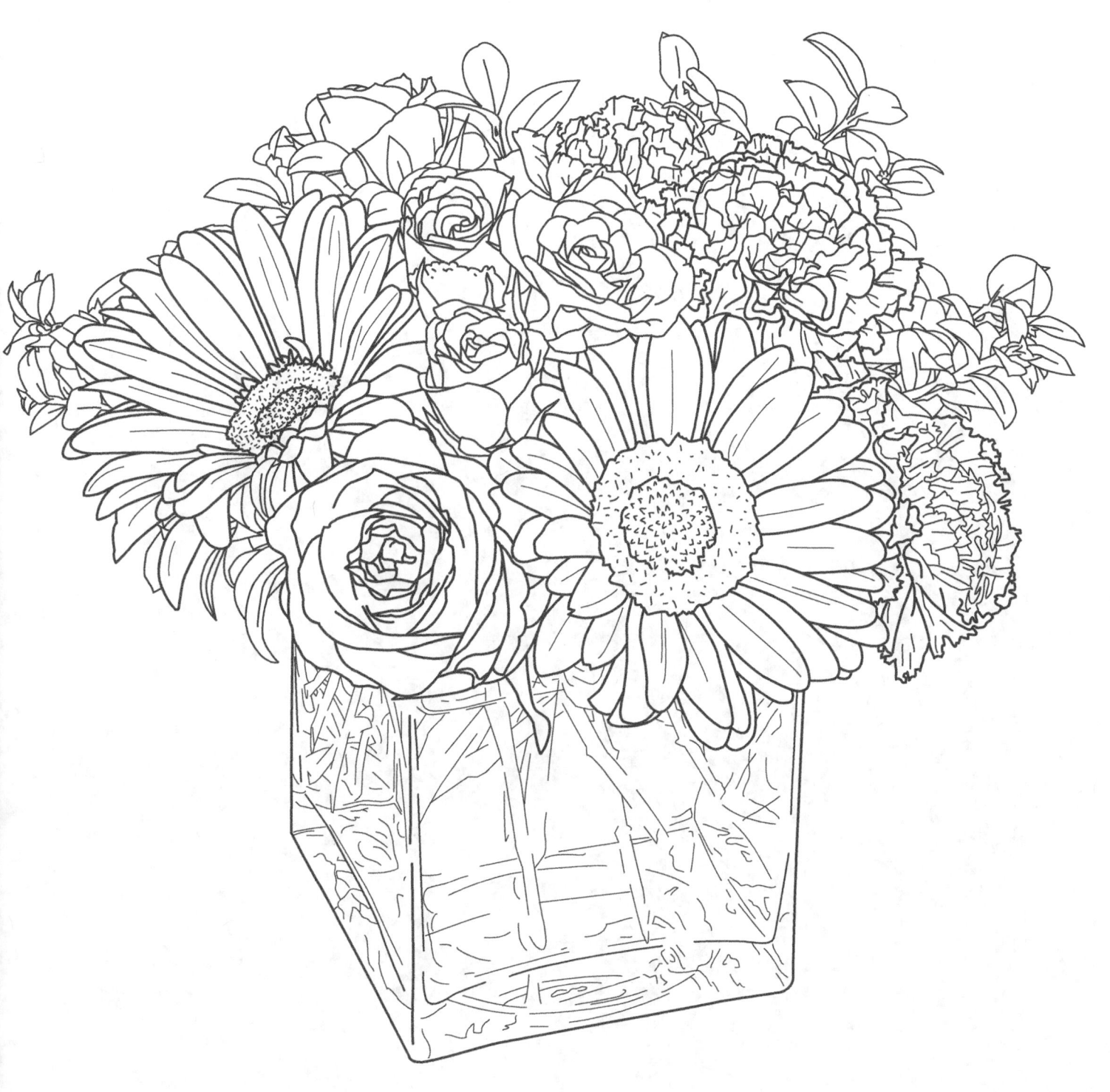

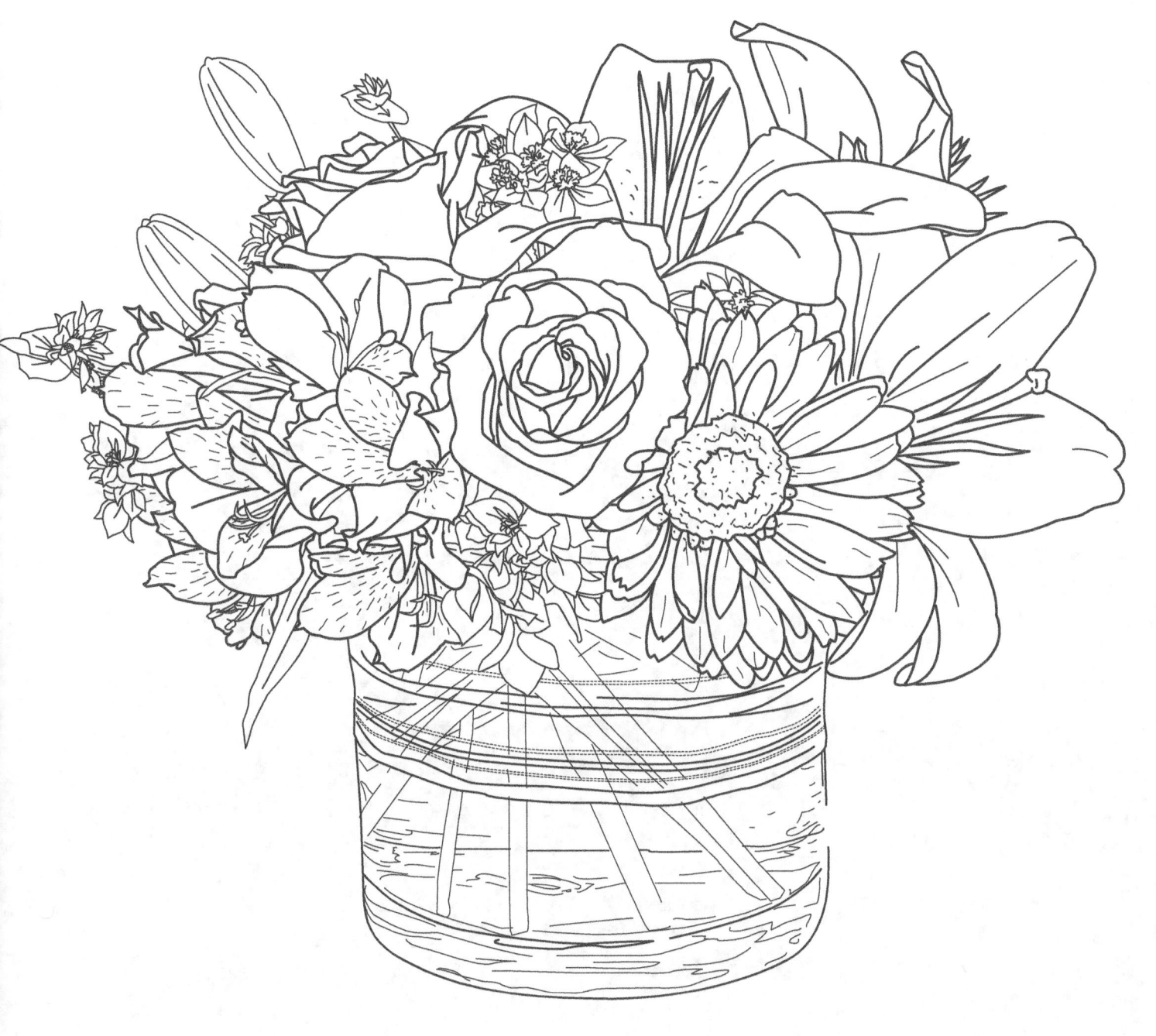

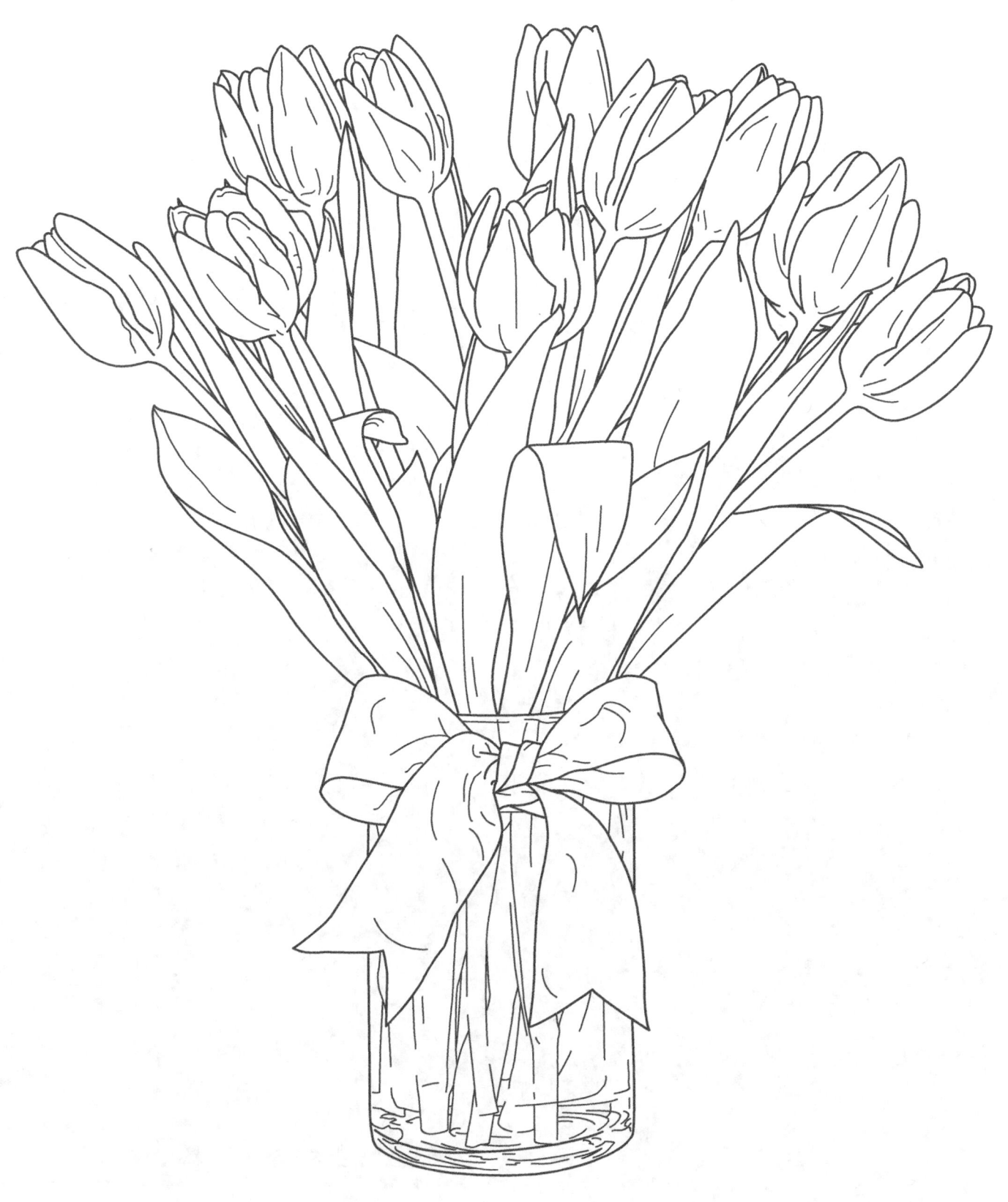

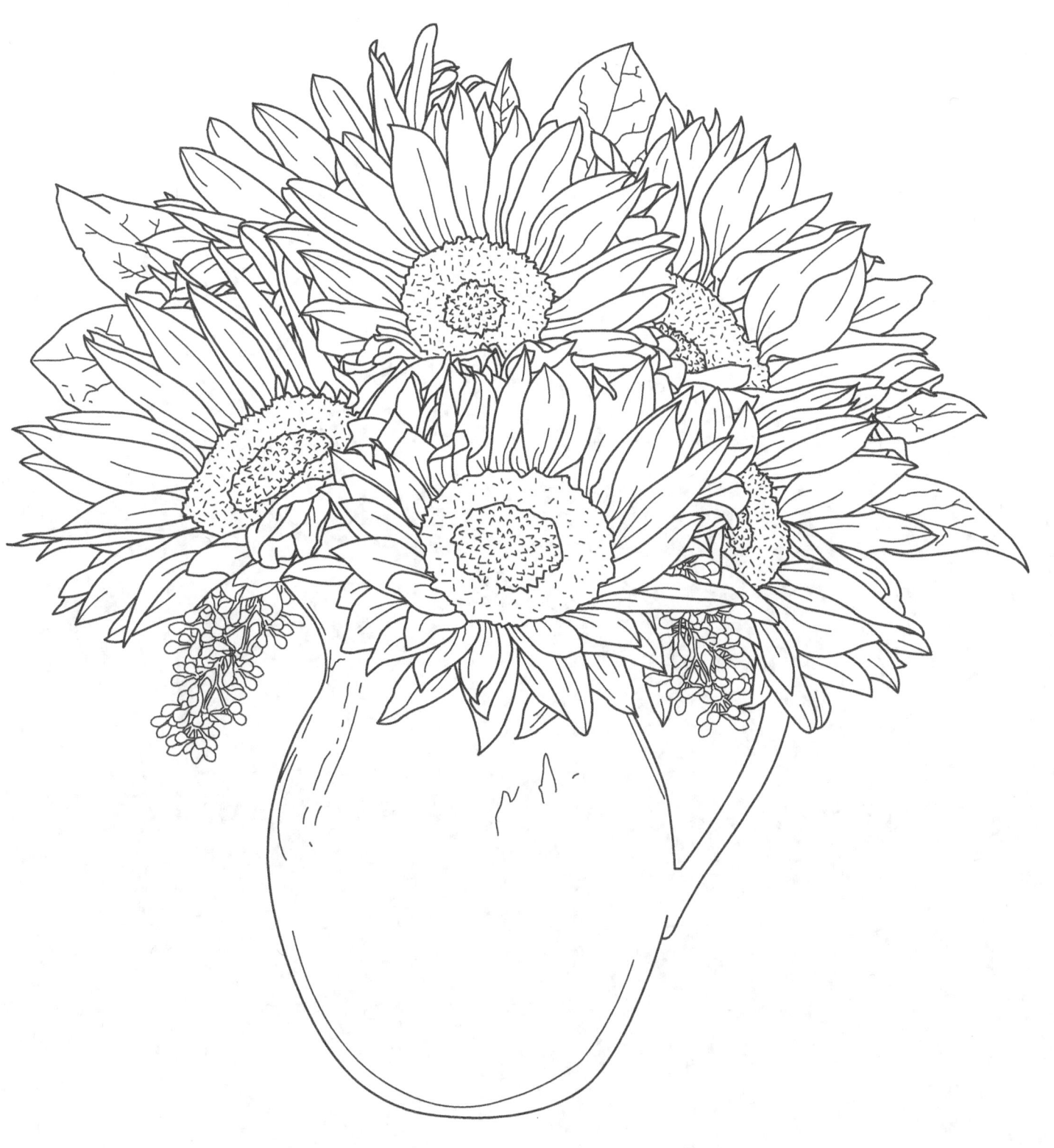

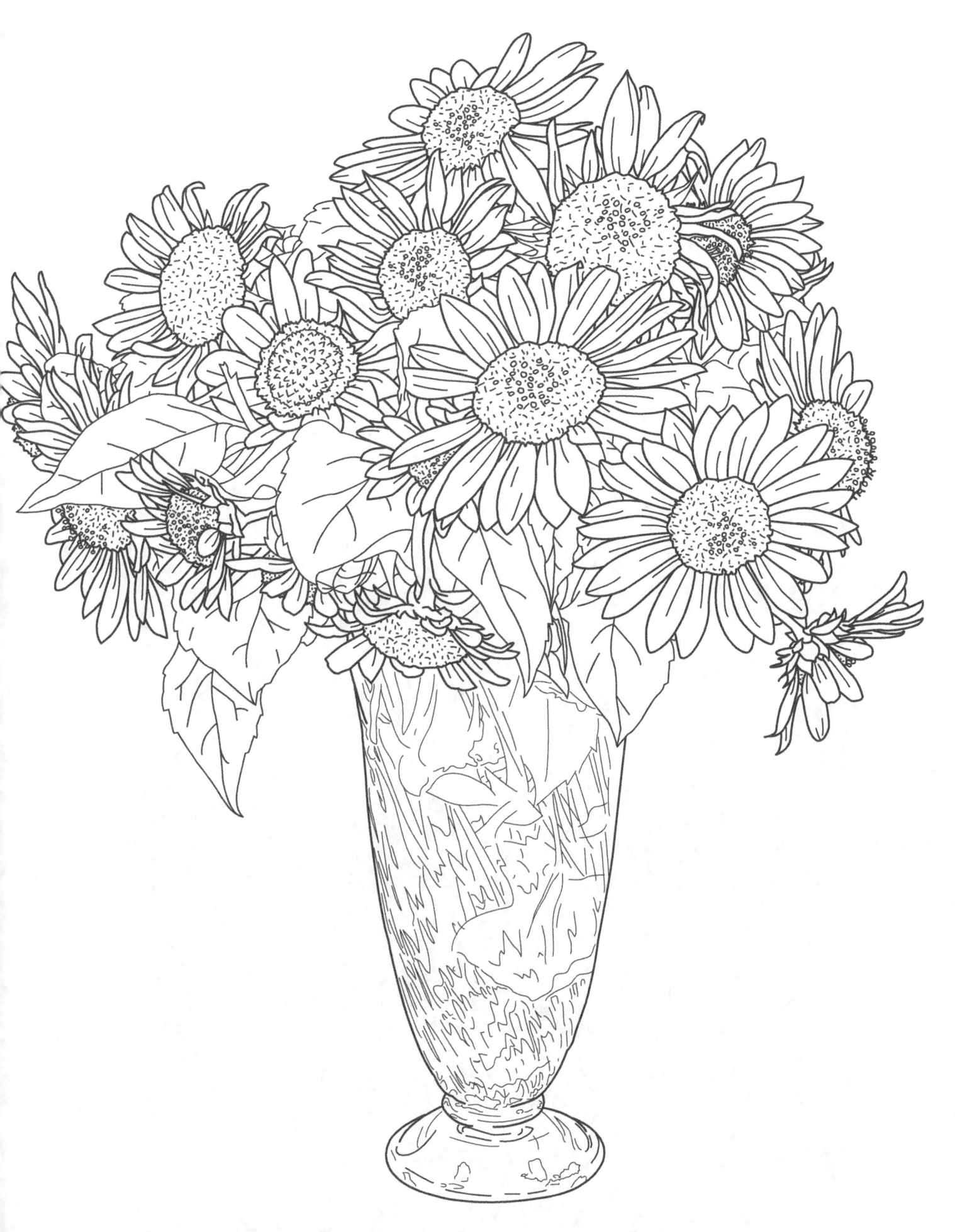

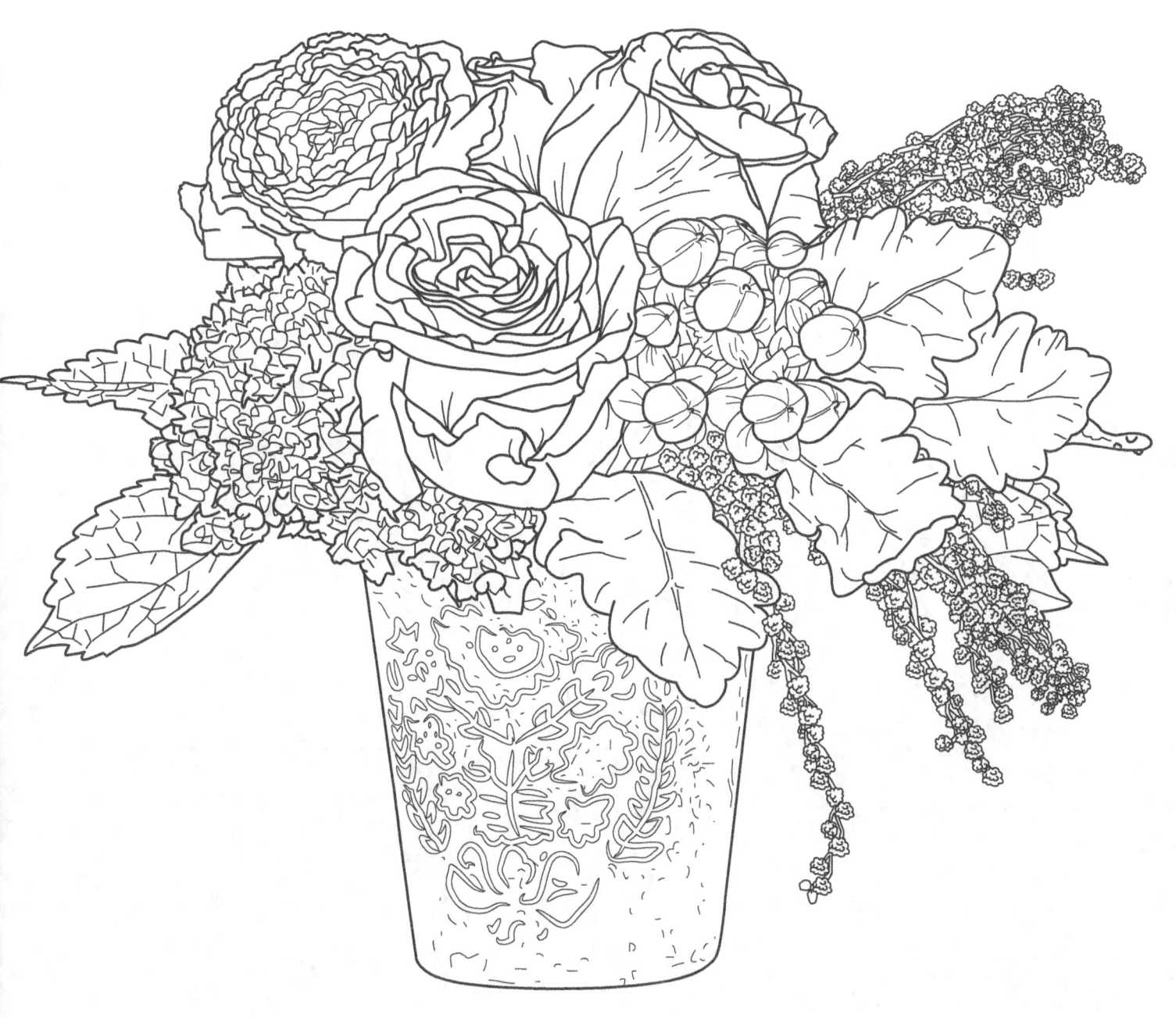

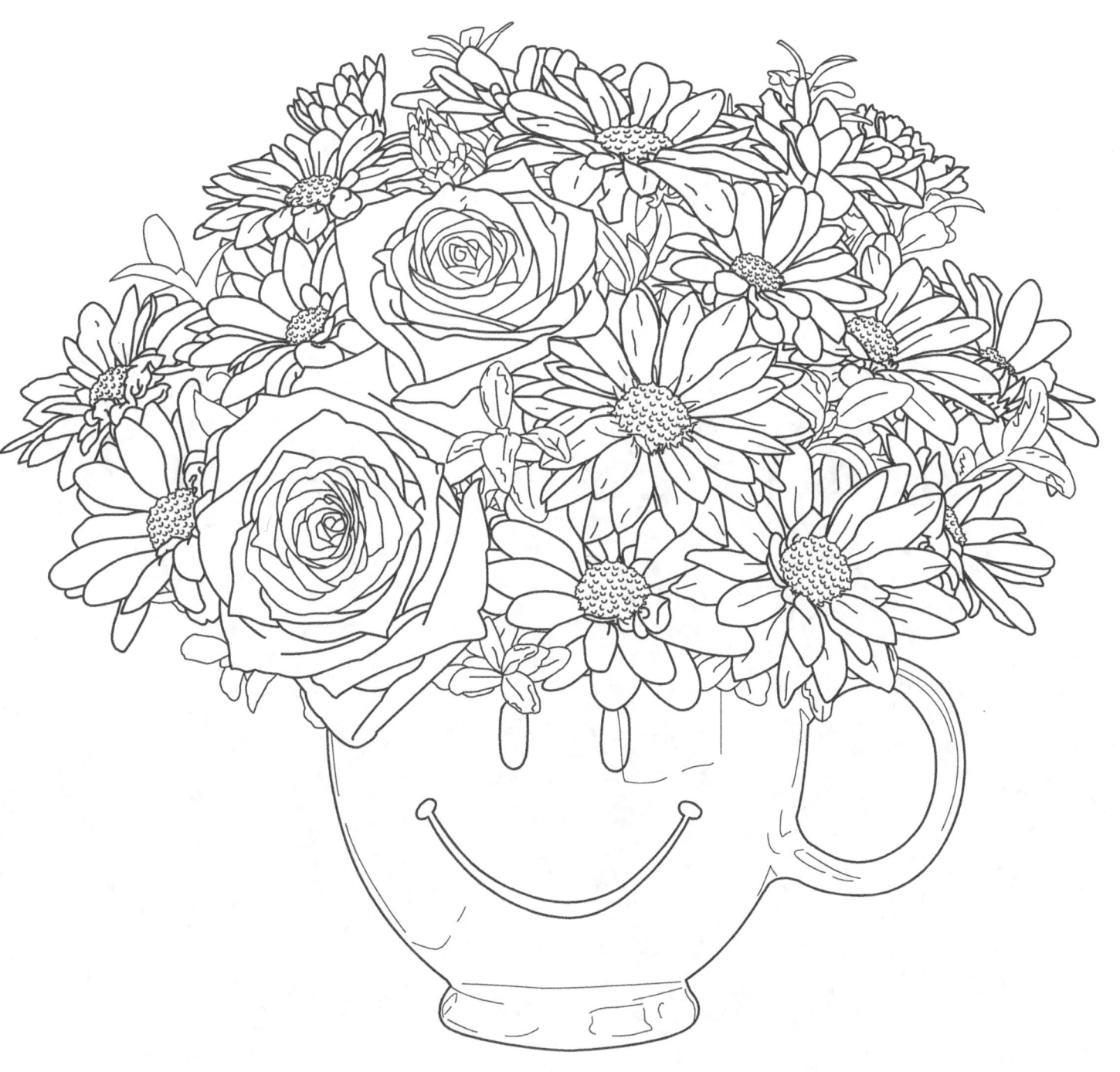

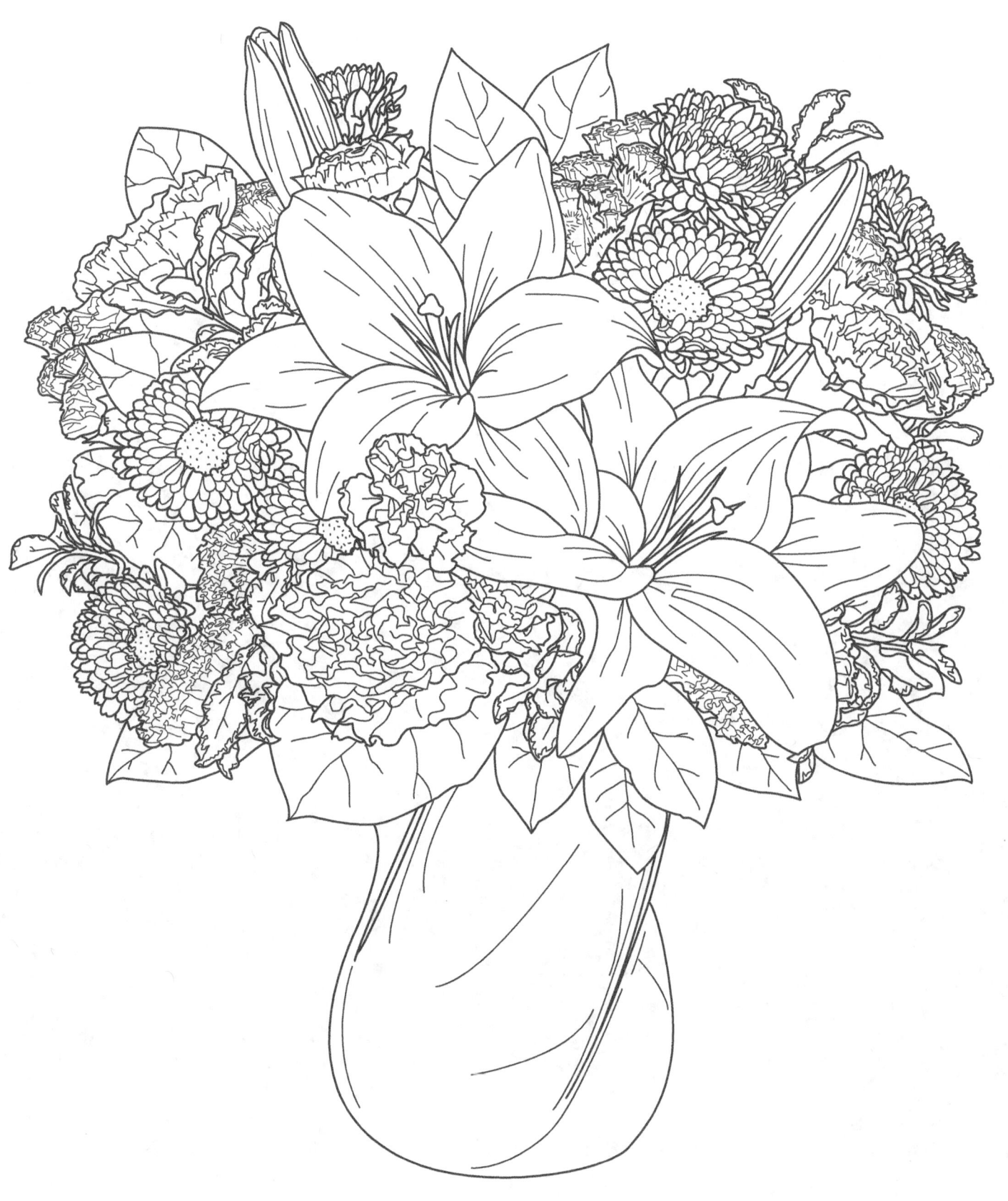

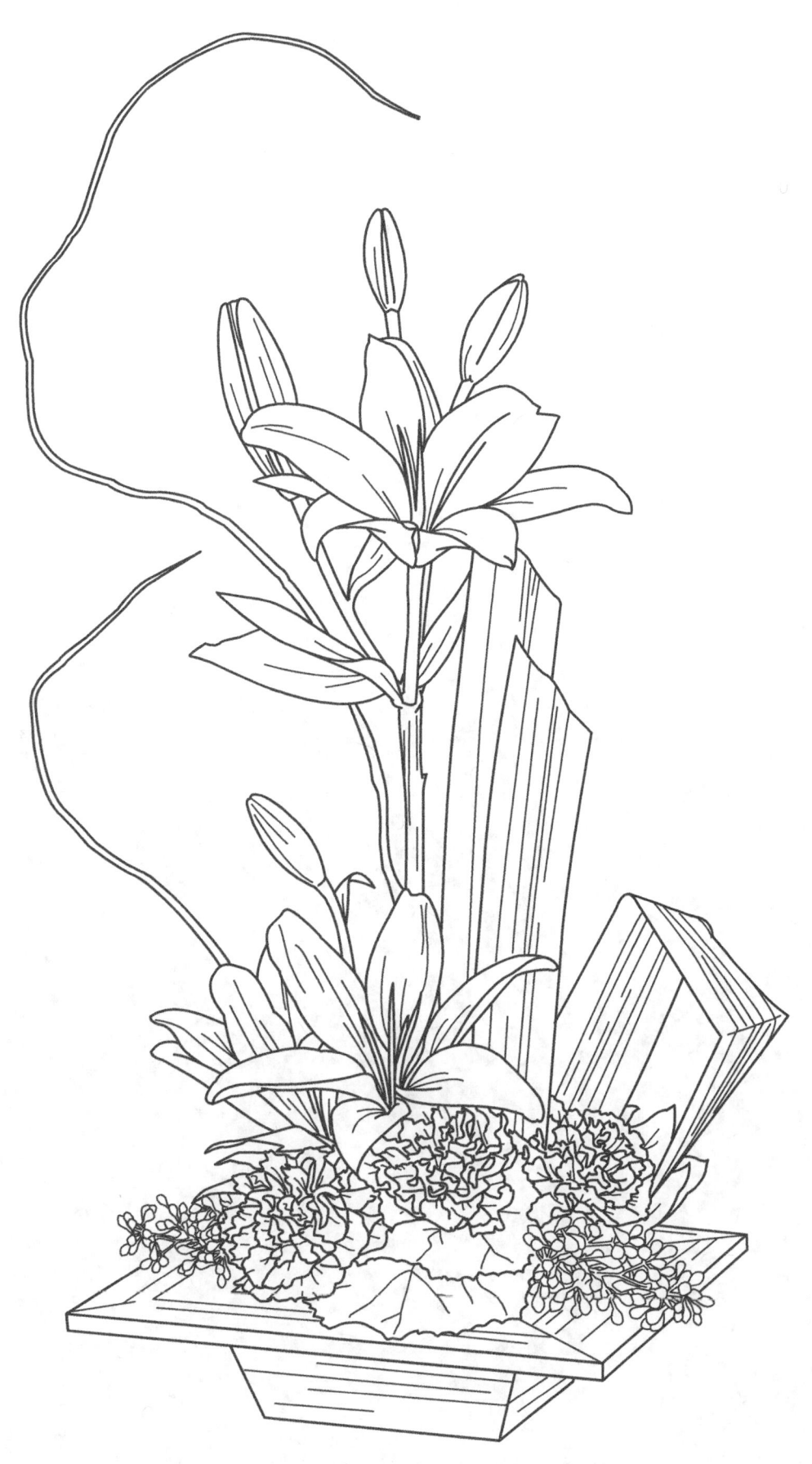

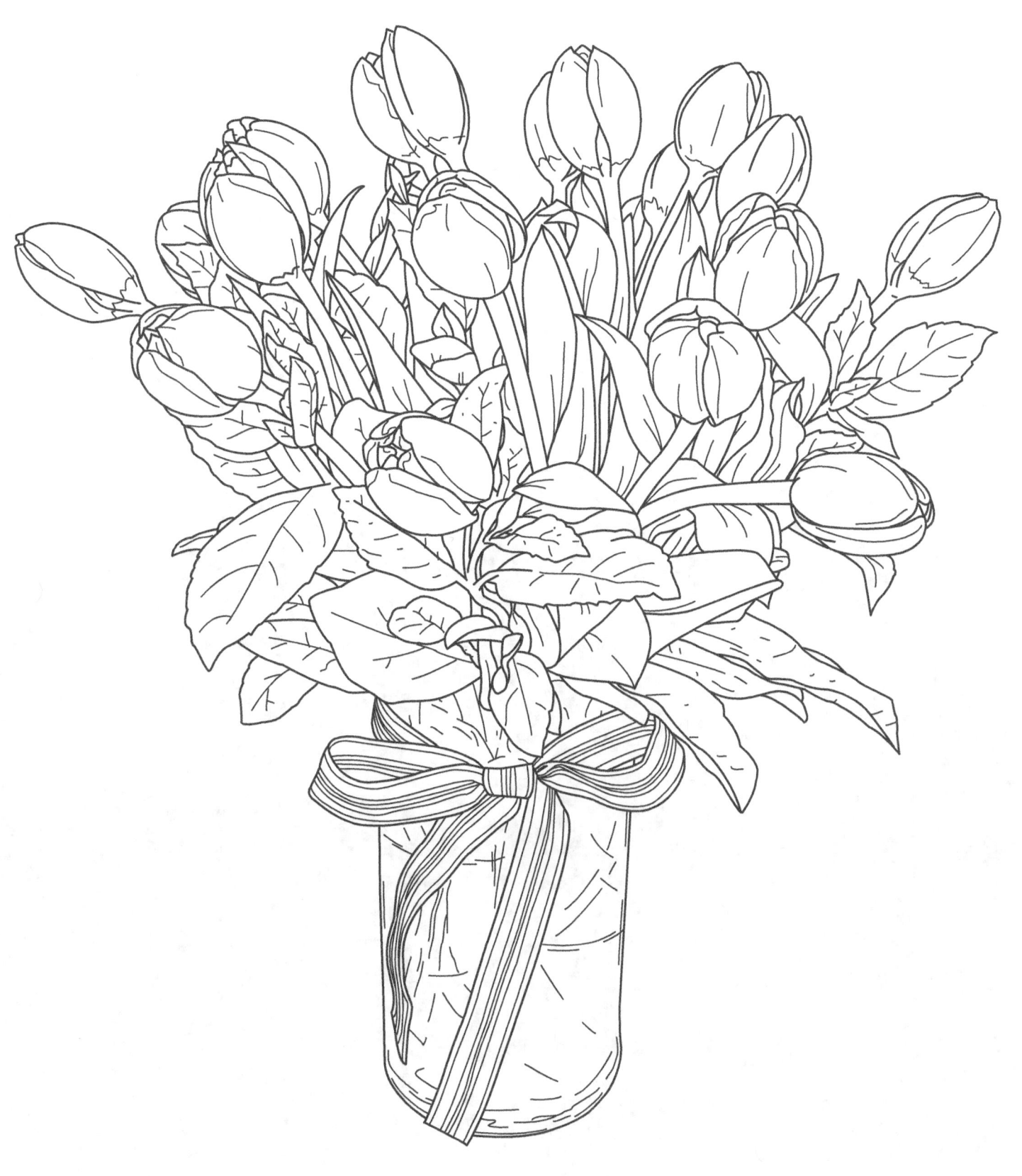

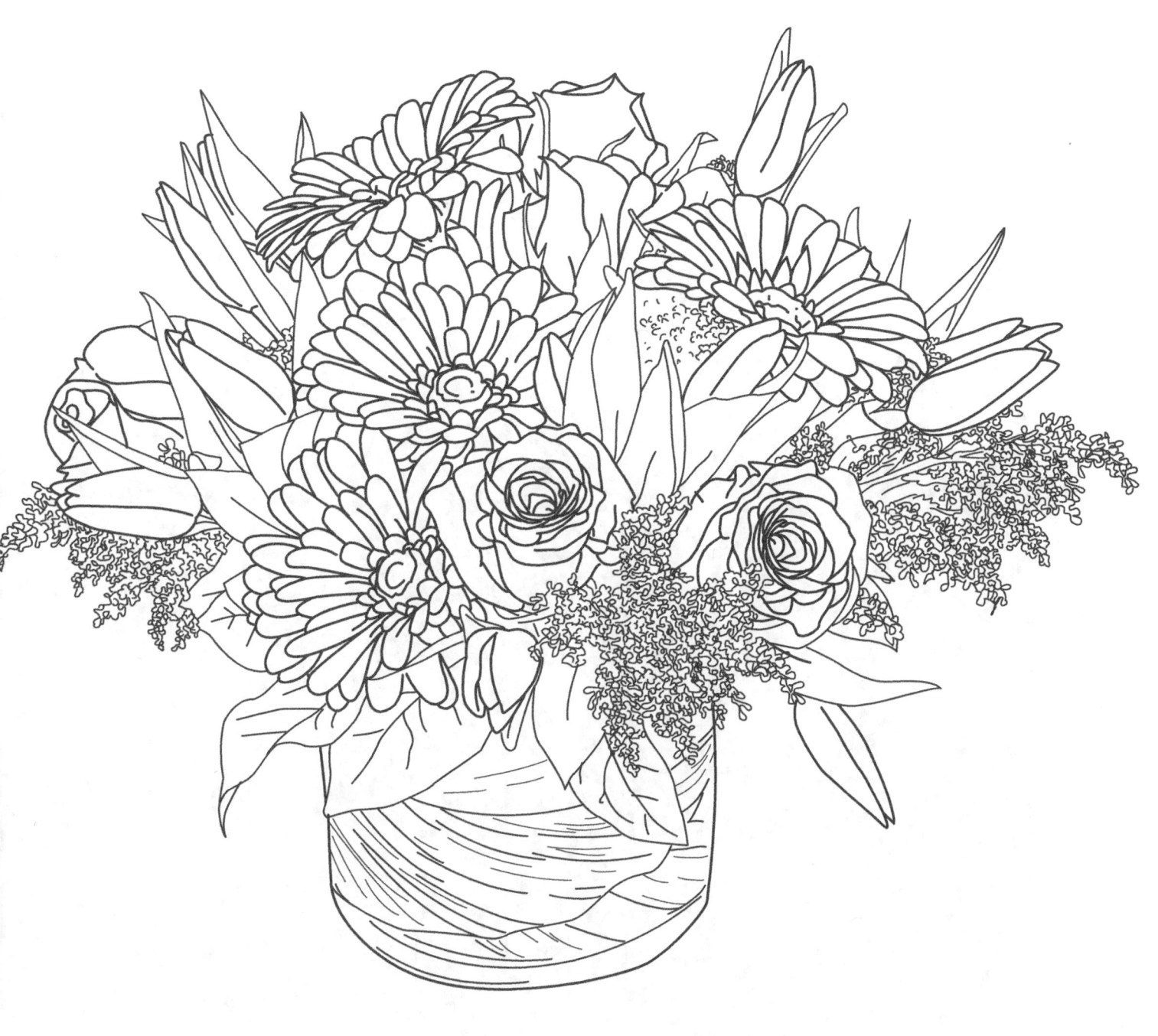

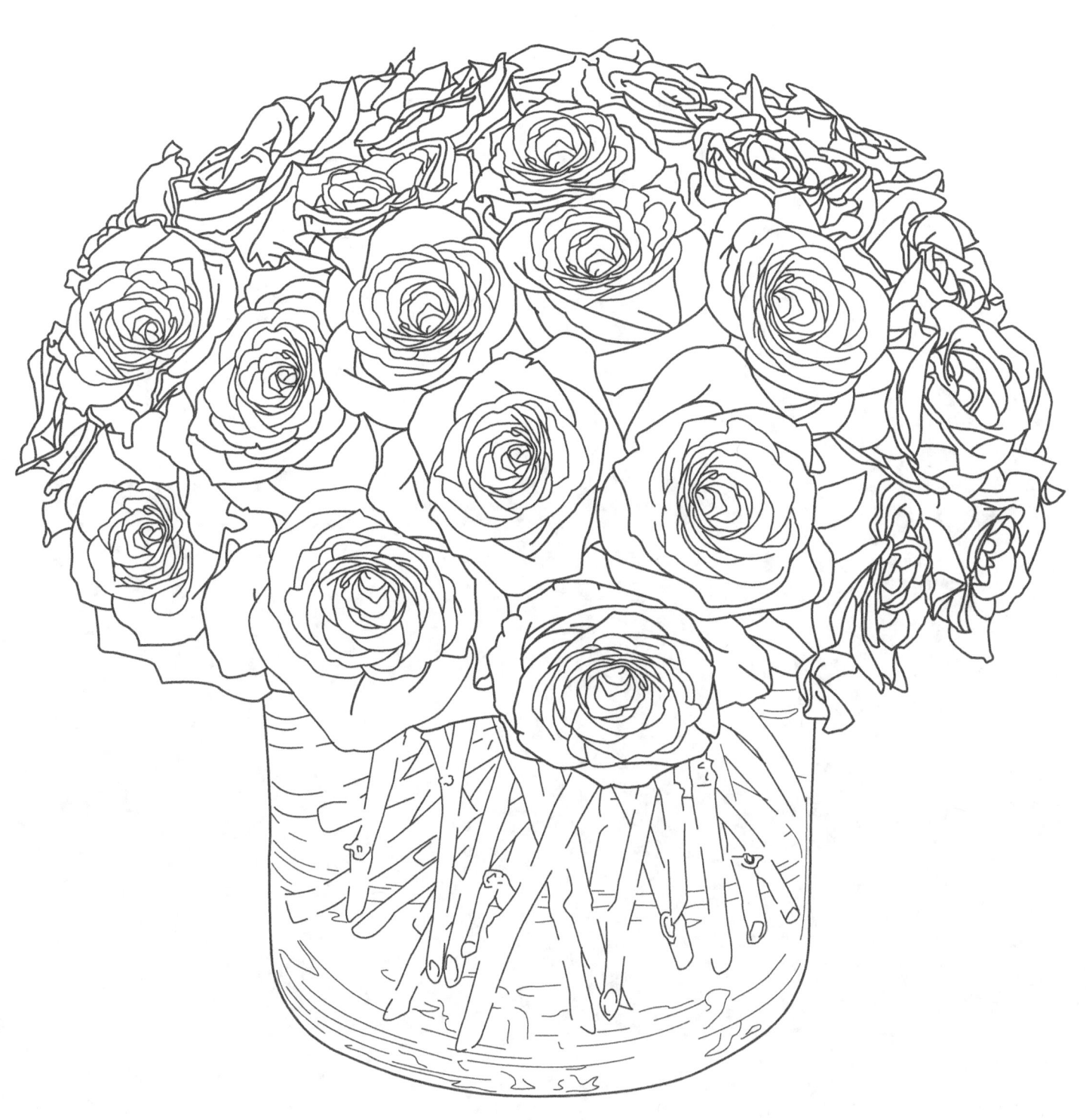

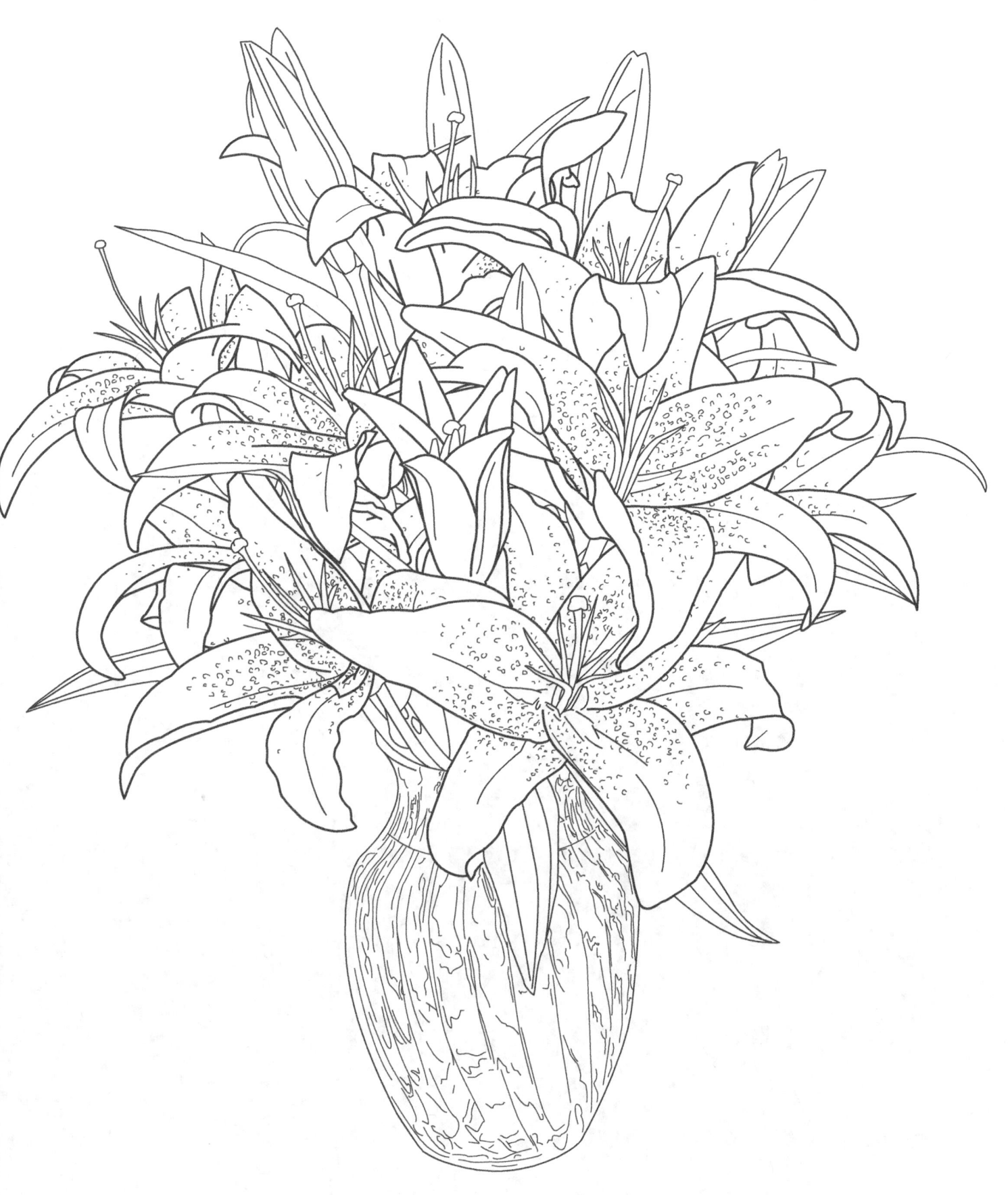

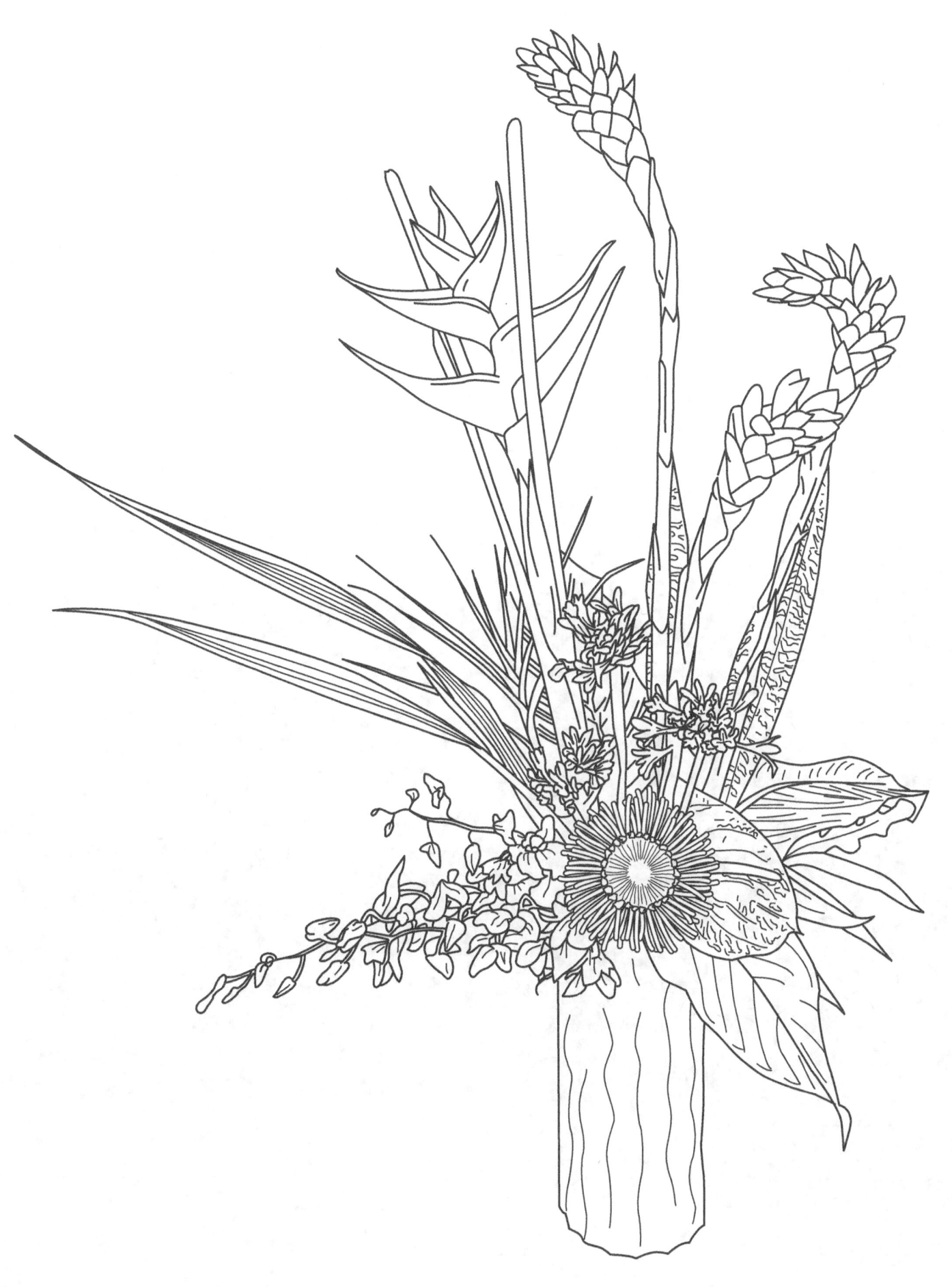

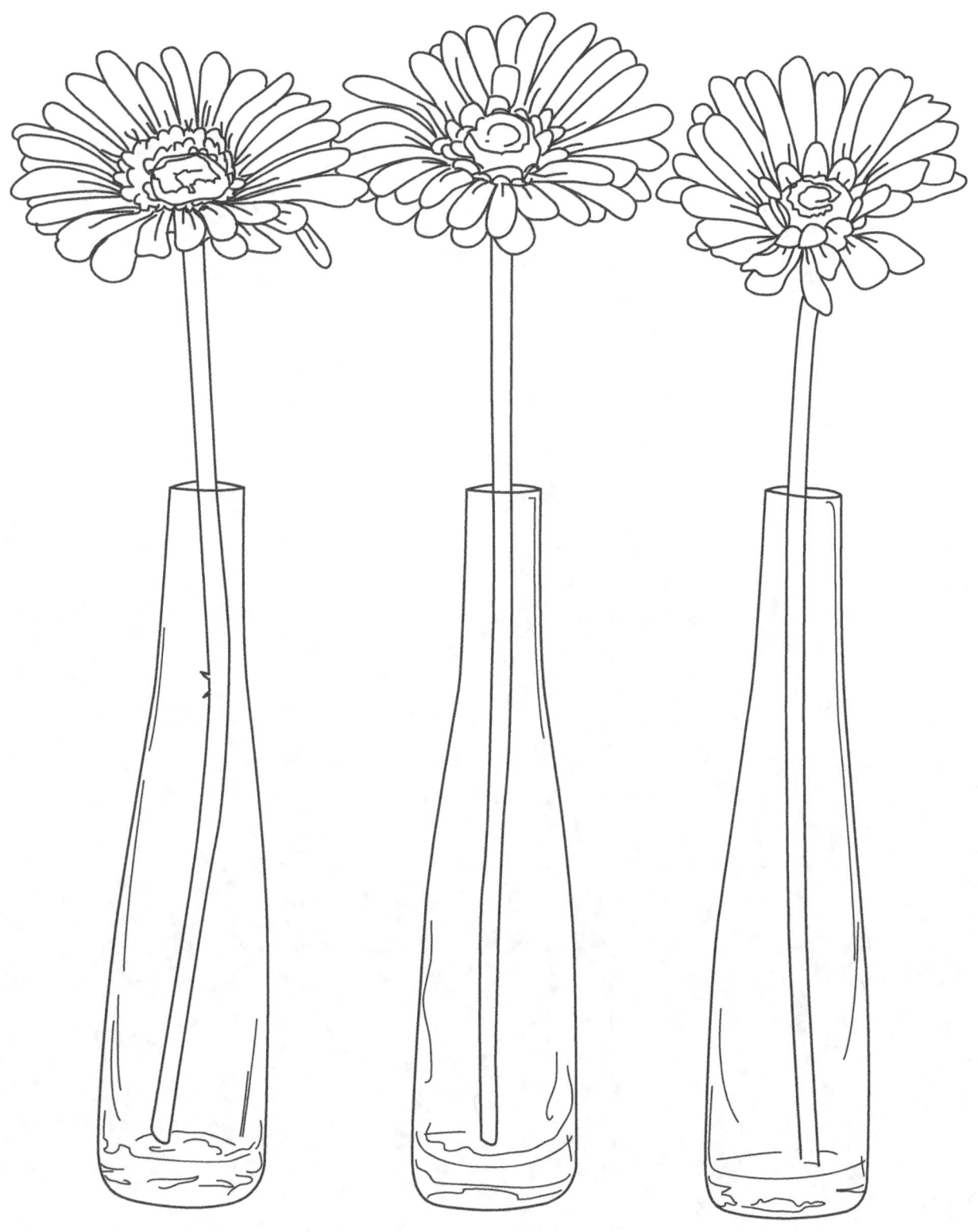

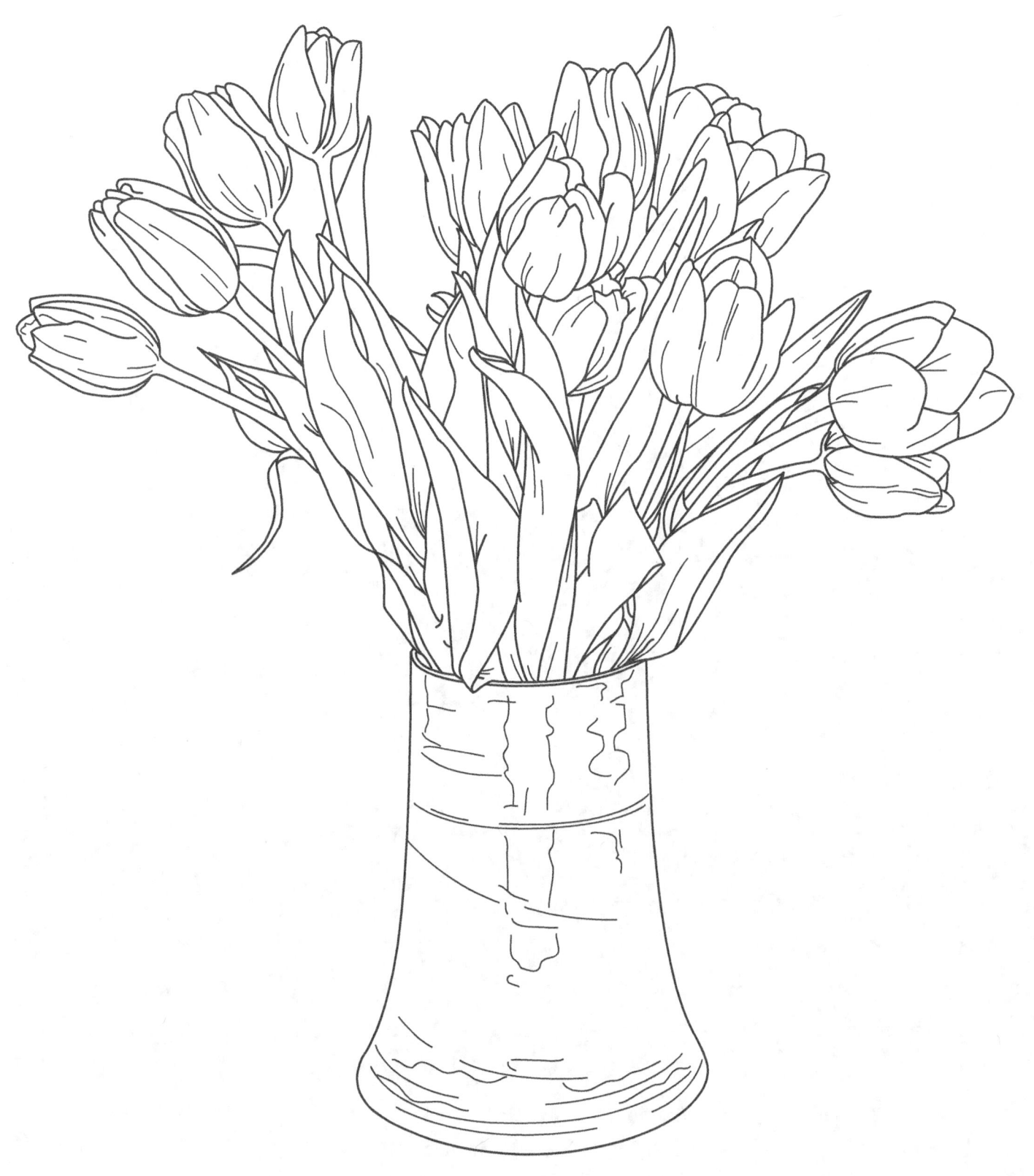

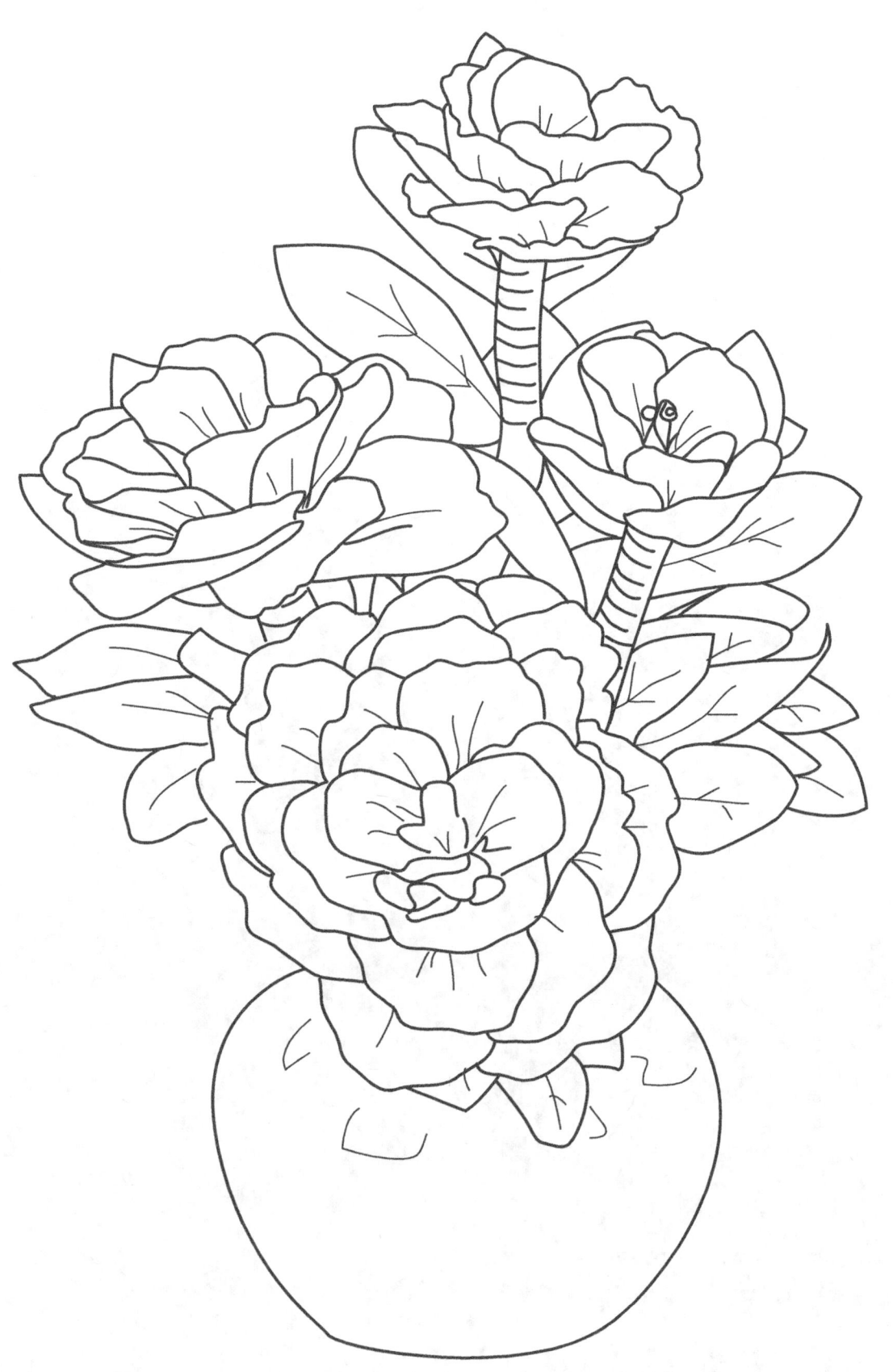

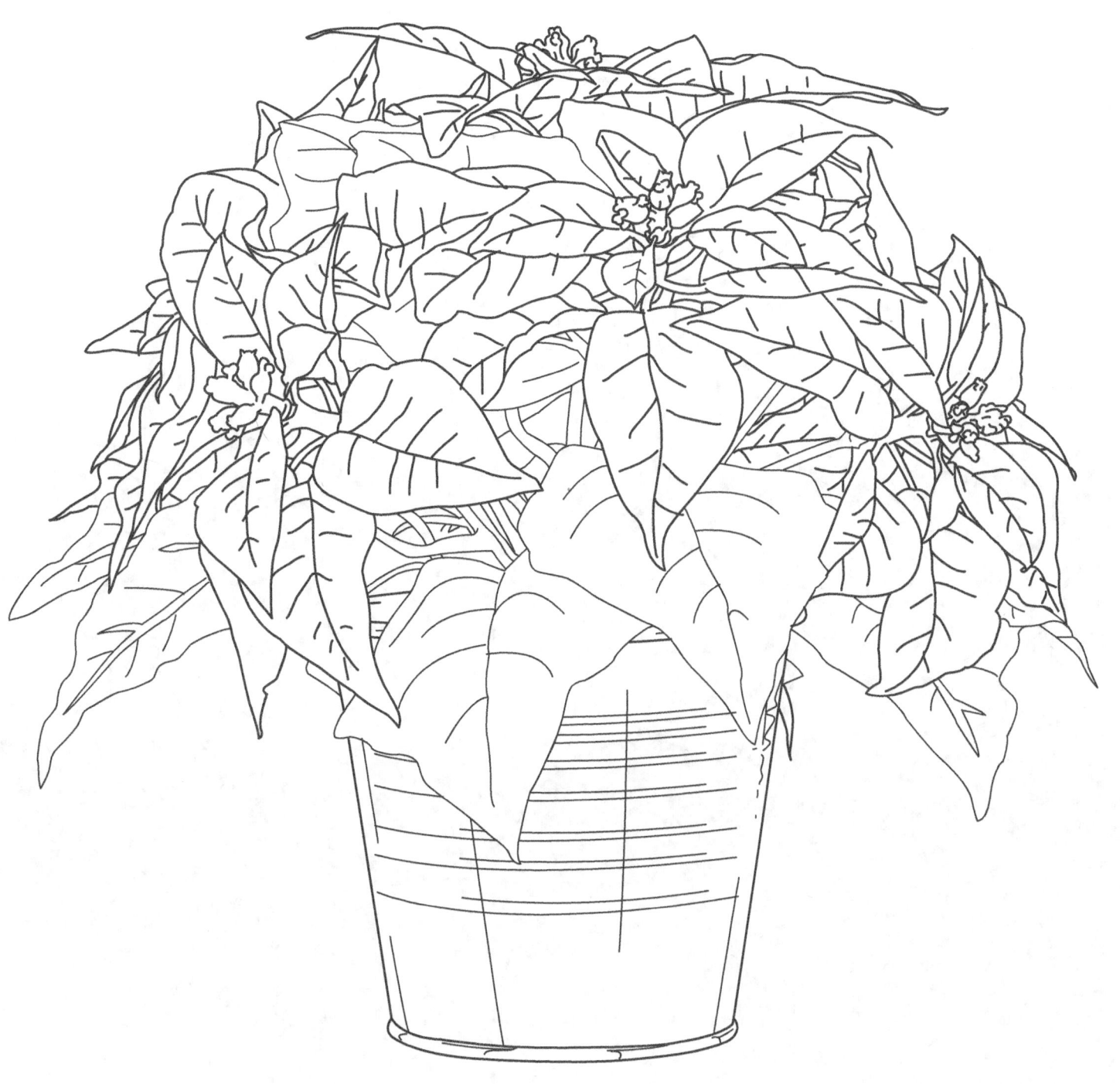

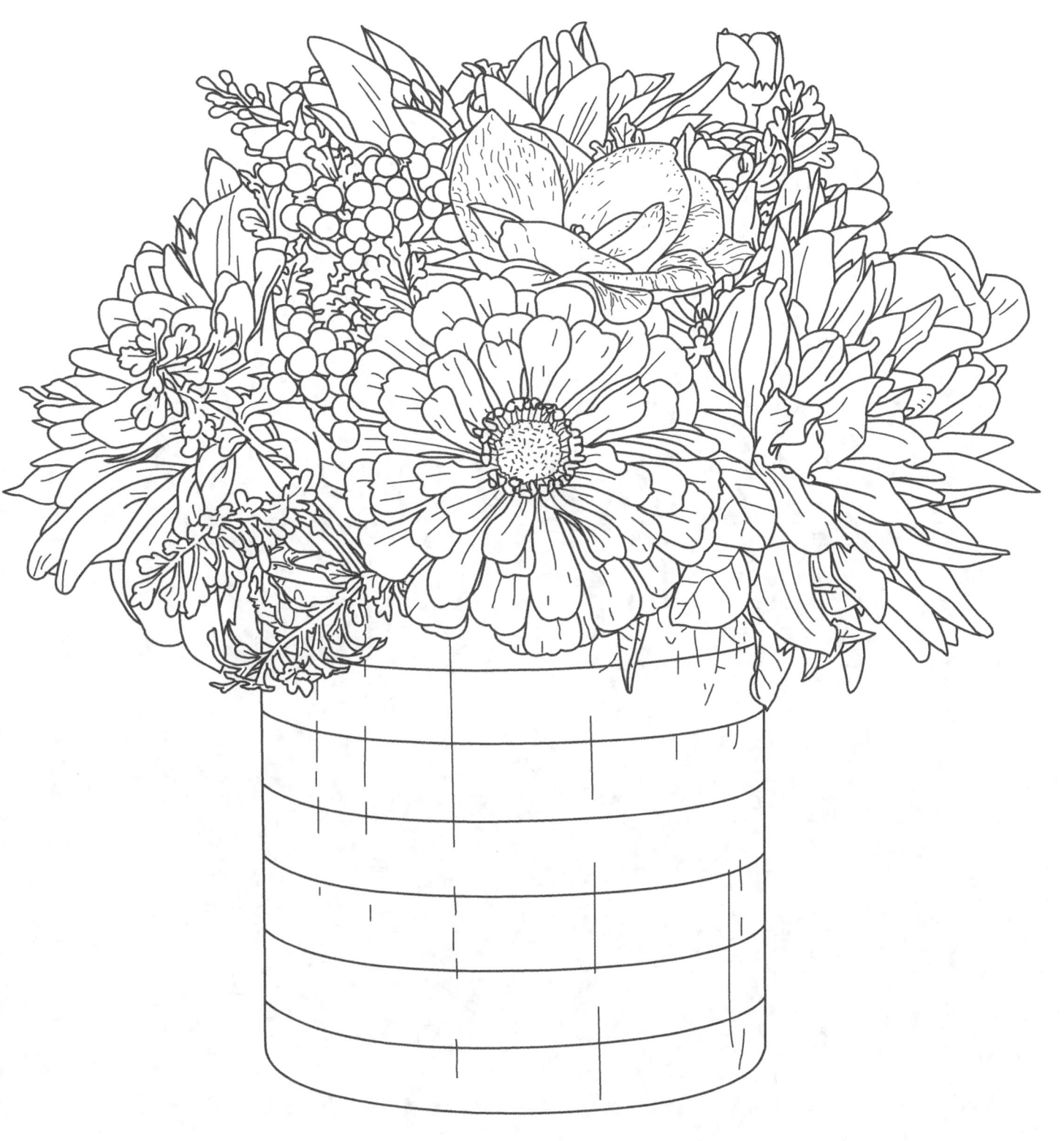

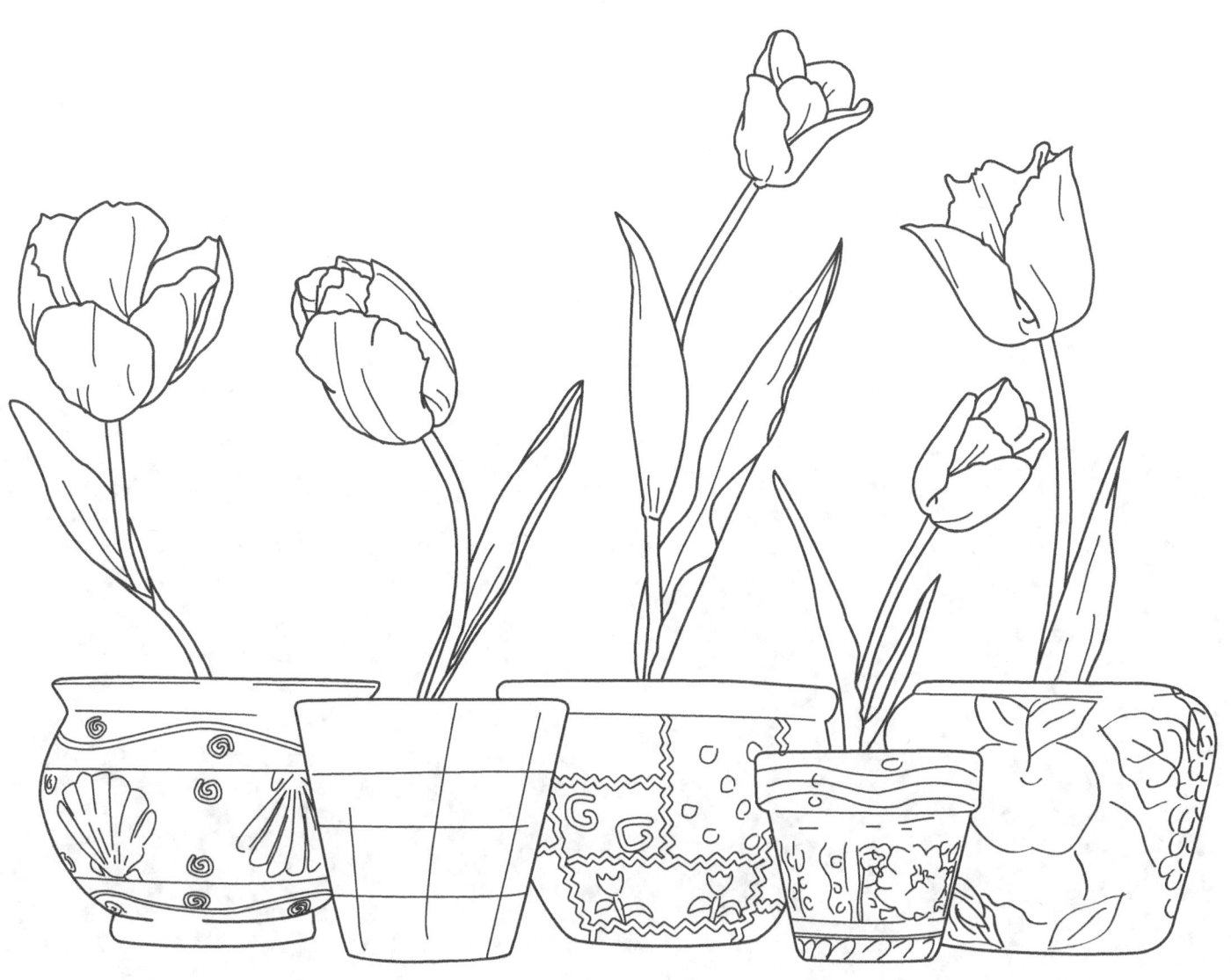

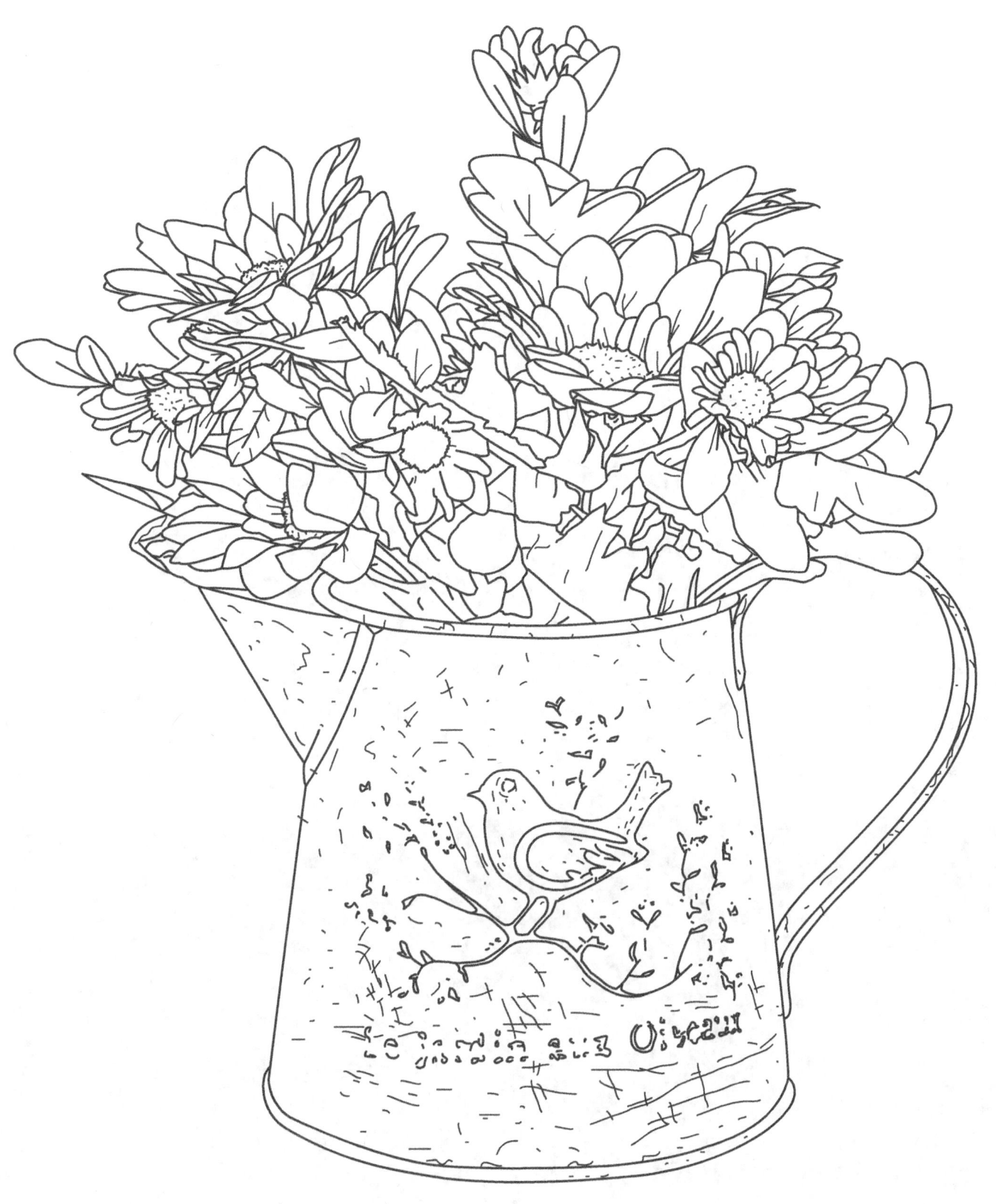

Be sure to look for other books by

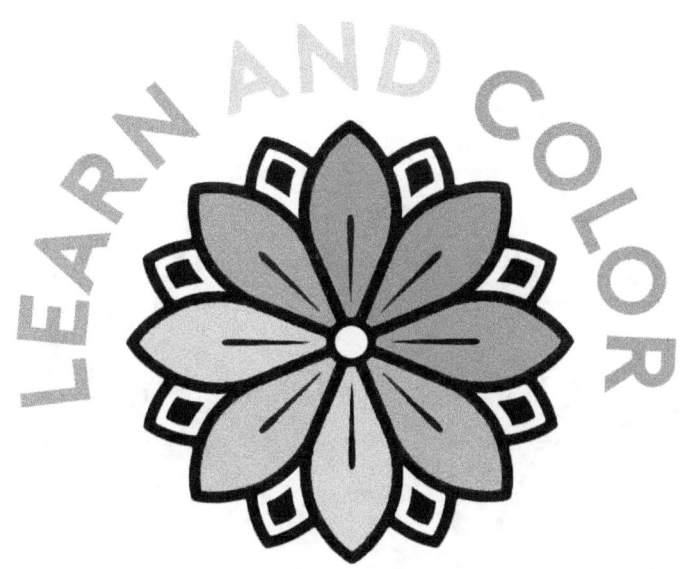